THE PHILOSOPHY OF
PHYSICAL SCIENCE

THE PHILOSOPHY OF
PHYSICAL SCIENCE

by

SIR ARTHUR EDDINGTON

ANN ARBOR PAPERBACKS

The University of Michigan Press

Third printing 1974
First edition as an Ann Arbor Paperback 1958
All rights reserved
ISBN 0–472–06020–1
First published by the Cambridge University Press
Reprinted by special arrangement
Published in the United States of America by
The University of Michigan Press and simultaneously
in Don Mills, Canada, by Longman Canada Limited
Manufactured in the United States of America

CONTENTS

PREFACE

THIS book contains the substance of the course of lectures which I delivered as Tarner Lecturer of Trinity College Cambridge in the Easter Term 1938. The lectures have afforded me an opportunity of developing more fully than in my earlier books the principles of philosophic thought associated with the modern advances of physical science.

It is often said that there is no "philosophy of science", but only the philosophies of certain scientists. But in so far as we recognise an authoritative body of opinion which decides what is and what is not accepted as present-day physics, there is an ascertainable present-day philosophy of physical science. It is the philosophy to which those who follow the accepted practice of science stand committed by their *practice*. It is implicit in the methods by which they advance science, sometimes without fully understanding why they employ them, and in the procedure which they accept as giving assurance of truth, often without examining what kind of assurance it can give.

There should be no conflict between the claim that a philosophy is scientifically grounded and the claim that it is, so far as it goes, a true philosophy. But in a specialised work of this kind the primary object must be to ascertain and discuss the philosophy which, whether true or not, is the present philosophy of physical science in the sense stated above. Those of us who believe that science, notwithstanding continual failures and readjustments, is slowly drawing nearer to the truth, are content that philosophic truth should be reached by the same method of progressive advance.

In order to make sure of our scientific foundations it is found necessary to enter rather deeply into the principles of relativity theory and quantum theory. Since the intention is to give, not merely an exposition, but a justification of the views to which they lead, some parts of the book introduce matters of considerable technical difficulty. Generally I have abstained from mathematical formulae; this, however, is not wholly out of consideration for the general reader, but because those whose minds are too much immersed in mathematical formulae are likely to miss what we are here seeking.

The discussion, although relating to the same subject matter, is mainly on different lines from that given eleven years ago in *The Nature of the Physical World*. The starting point in the present treatment is *knowledge*. The title of the earlier book might have been expanded into "the nature of the physical universe, with applications to the theory of physical knowledge"; the corresponding title of the present book would be "the nature of physical knowledge, with applications to the theory of the physical universe". The change of emphasis makes for a more logical sequence of ideas; but primarily it reflects a change which has occurred in physical science itself. It is significant of this change that the contrast between the scientific table and the familiar table, with which *The Nature of the Physical World* opens, had become a contrast between the scientific story and the familiar story of experience at the beginning of *New Pathways in Science*. The first was, I believe, the natural form of expression according to the scientific outlook of 1928; the second had become more natural six years later.

Neither the scientific advances of the last decade nor the years of reflection have altered the general trend of my philosophy. I say "my philosophy", not as claiming authorship of ideas which are widely diffused in modern thought, but because the ultimate selection and synthesis must be a personal responsibility. If it were necessary to give a short name to this philosophy, I should hesitate between "Selective subjectivism" and "Structuralism". The former name refers to the aspect most prominent in the first eight chapters; the latter refers to a more mathematical conception which dominates the rest of the book. Both can now be carried much farther than in *The Nature of the Physical World*. The domain of subjectivity has been extended as a consequence of our better understanding of quantum mechanics; and the conception of structure has been made more precise by the connection now recognised between the foundations of physics and the mathematical Theory of Groups.

With this "philosophy of physical science" as a nucleus, I endeavour in the last two chapters to develop the outline of a general philosophical outlook which a scientist can accept without inconsistency. I am not among those who think that in the search for truth all aspects of human experience are to be ignored save those which are followed up in physical science. But I find no disharmony between a philosophy which embraces the wider significance of human experience and the specialised philosophy of physical science, even though the latter relates to a system of thought of recent growth whose stability is yet to be tested.

A. S. E

CAMBRIDGE
April 1939

CHAPTER I

SCIENTIFIC EPISTEMOLOGY

I

BETWEEN physics and philosophy there lies a debatable territory which I shall call *scientific epistemology*. Epistemology is that branch of philosophy which treats of the nature of knowledge. It will not be denied that a significant part of the whole field of knowledge is that which has come to us by the methods of physical science. This part takes the form of a detailed description of a world—the so-called physical universe. I give the name "scientific epistemology" to the sub-branch of epistemology which deals with the nature of this part of our knowledge, and therefore indirectly with the nature and status of the physical universe to which it formally relates.

There are two matters of definition which it is desirable to make clear at the outset.

Some writers restrict the term "knowledge" to things of which we are quite certain; others recognise knowledge of varying degrees of uncertainty. This is one of the common ambiguities of speech as to which no one is entitled to dictate, and an author can only state which usage he has himself chosen to follow. If "to know" means "to be quite certain of", the term is of little use to those who wish to be undogmatic. I therefore prefer the broader meaning; and my own usage will recognise uncertain knowledge. Anything which would be knowledge if we were assured of its truth, is still counted as knowledge (uncertain or false knowledge) if we are not assured.

It will not be necessary for us to formulate a general definition of knowledge. Our procedure will be to specify

a particular collection of more or less widely accepted knowledge, and then to make an epistemological study of its
nature. Especially, though not exclusively, we have to
consider the knowledge acquired by the methods of physical
science. For brevity I will call this *physical knowledge*. In
principle we might identify physical knowledge with the
contents of certain encyclopaedic works, such as the *Hand-
buch der Physik*, which between them cover the various
branches of physical science. But there are obvious objections to a slavish acceptance of a particular authority;
and I will therefore define physical knowledge to be that
which a right-thinking person* would to-day accept as
justified by physical science.

It should not be overlooked that physical knowledge
includes a vast amount of miscellaneous information which
would be out of place in scientific text-books. For example,
the result of a measurement of weight is physical knowledge,
whether it is made for the purpose of deciding a scientific
issue or for deciding the amount of a tradesman's bill. The
condition is that it shall be passed as scientifically correct (by
the right-thinking person), not that it shall be scientifically
important. It should also be noticed that the term is intended
to refer to physical science as it stands to-day. We are not
going to occupy ourselves with speculations as to possible
future developments. We are to take stock of the results
which the methods of physical science have yielded up to
now, and see what kind of knowledge we have been acquiring.

I have said that I do not regard the term "knowledge" as
implying assurance of truth. But in considering a particular
body of knowledge, it may be assumed that an effort has
been made to admit to that body only the more trustworthy
knowledge; so that usually a reasonable degree of certainty

* "Right-thinking person" is, of course, a modest way of referring
to oneself.

or probability is attributable to the knowledge which we shall have occasion to discuss. But the assessment of certainty of knowledge is to be regarded as separate from the study of the nature of knowledge.

The other matter of definition is the term "physical universe". Physical knowledge (as accepted and formulated to-day) has the form of a description of a world. We *define* the physical universe to be the world so described. Effectively therefore the physical universe is defined as the theme of a specified body of knowledge, just as Mr Pickwick might be defined as the hero of a specified novel.

A great advantage of this definition is that it does not prejudge the question whether the physical universe—or Mr Pickwick—really exists. That is left open for discussion if we can agree on a definition of "really exists", which for most persons is a parrot-phrase whose meaning they have not troubled to consider. The few who have attempted to give it a definite meaning do not always agree on the meaning. By defining the physical universe and the physical objects which constitute it as the theme of a specified body of knowledge, and not as things possessing a property of existence elusive of definition, we free the foundations of physics from suspicion of metaphysical contamination.

This type of definition is characteristic of the epistemological approach, which takes knowledge as the starting point rather than an existent entity of which we have somehow to obtain knowledge. But in defining scientifically a term already in common use, we must be careful to avoid abuse of language. To justify the above definition of the physical universe, we ought to show that it is not in conflict with what the ordinary man (in which term I do not include philosophers) understands by the physical universe. This justification is deferred to p. 159.

II

The nature of physical knowledge and of the world which it professes to describe has long been a battleground for rival schools of philosophers. But physicists can scarcely be denied a hearing on a subject which concerns them so intimately. A student of physical science should be in a position to throw some light on the nature of the knowledge obtainable by the methods which he practises. Recently a number of books have been written by authors whose qualifications are purely scientific, in which scientific epistemology is developed and used as an approach to the wider problems of philosophy. I do not think that this "intrusion" into philosophy is a matter for surprise or caustic comment.

One often finds an impression that it is an innovation for scientists to indulge in philosophy; but this is incorrect. I have noticed that some of the recent books are plentifully sprinkled with quotations from scientists of the nineteenth century which, whether they fortify the argument or not, prove at any rate that our predecessors shared the common foible of holding strong philosophic views—and expressing them. Some were out of their depth, then as now. But some were profound thinkers—Clifford, Karl Pearson, Poincaré, and others—whose writings have an honoured place in the development of scientific philosophy.

It is, however, important to recognise that about twenty-five years ago the invasion of philosophy by physics assumed a different character. Up till then traffic with philosophy had been a luxury for those scientists whose disposition happened to turn that way. I can find no indication that the scientific researches of Pearson and Poincaré were in any way inspired or guided by their particular philosophical outlook. They had no opportunity to put their philosophy into practice. Conversely, their philosophical conclusions were the outcome of general scientific training, and were not to any extent dependent on familiarity with recondite investigations and theories. To advance science and to philosophise on science were essentially distinct activities. In the new movement scientific epistemology is much more intimately associated with science. For developing the modern theories of matter and radiation a definite epistemological outlook has become a necessity; and it is the direct source of the most far-reaching scientific advances.

We have discovered that *it is actually an aid in the search for knowledge to understand the nature of the knowledge which we seek.*

By making practical application of our epistemological conclusions we subject them to the same kind of observational control as physical hypotheses. If our epistemology is at fault, it will lead to an *impasse* in the scientific developments proceeding from it; that warns us that our philosophical insight has not been deep enough, and we must cast about to find what has been overlooked. In this way scientific advances which result from epistemological insight have in turn educated our epistemological insight. Between science and scientific epistemology there has been a give and take by which both have greatly benefited.

In the view of scientists at least, this observational control gives to modern scientific epistemology a security which philosophy has not usually been able to attain. It introduces also the same kind of progressive development which is characteristic of science, but not hitherto of philosophy. We are not making a series of shots at ultimate truth, which may hit or miss. What we claim for the present system of scientific philosophy is that it is an advance on that which went before, and that it is a foundation for the advances which will come after it.

In science the observational test is valuable, not only for controlling physical hypotheses (for which it is indeed the only possible guarantee), but also for detecting fallacies of argument and unwarranted assumptions. It is the latter kind of control that an observational test applies to scientific epistemology. This may seem superfluous to those who never reason incorrectly. But perhaps even the most confident philosopher will admit that there are some of his opponents to whom such control would be salutary. I have little doubt that every one of the philosophical conclusions in this book has been anticipated by one of the schools of philosophy—and emphatically condemned by another. But to those who recognise them as familiar truisms or as long-condemned fallacies, I would point out that they are now put forward with altogether new sanctions which ought to be reckoned with.

Theoretical physicists, through the inescapable demands of their own subject, have been forced to become epistemologists, just as pure mathematicians have been forced to become logicians. The invasion of the epistemological branch of philosophy by physics is exactly parallel to the invasion of the logical branch of philosophy by mathematics. Pure mathematicians, having learnt by experience that the obvious is difficult to prove—and not always true—found it necessary to delve into the foundations of their own processes of reasoning; in so doing they developed a powerful technique which has been welcomed for the advancement of logic generally. A similar pressure of necessity has caused physicists to enter into epistemology, rather against their will. Most of us, as plain men of science, begin with an aversion to the philosophic type of inquiry into the nature of things. Whether we are persuaded that the nature of physical objects is obvious to commonsense, or whether we are persuaded that it is inscrutable beyond human understanding, we are inclined to dismiss the inquiry as unpractical and futile. But modern physics has not been able to maintain this aloofness. There can be little doubt that its advances, though applying primarily to the restricted field of scientific epistemology, have a wider bearing, and offer an effective contribution to the philosophical outlook as a whole.

Formally we may still recognise a distinction between science, as treating the *content* of knowledge, and scientific epistemology, as treating the *nature* of knowledge of the physical universe. But it is no longer a practical partition; and to conform to the present situation scientific epistemology should be included in science. We do not dispute that it must also be included in philosophy. It is a field in which philosophy and physics overlap.

III

So long as a scientific writer on philosophy confines himself to scientific epistemology, he is not outside the borders of his own subject. But most authors have felt that they could usefully advance farther and consider the general philosophical bearing of the new conceptions. This venturesomeness has been strongly criticised; but it seems to me that the critics have failed to grasp the situation.

It is recorded that Archbishop Davidson, in conversation with Einstein, asked him what effect he thought the theory of relativity would have on religion. Einstein answered: "None. Relativity is a purely scientific theory, and has nothing to do with religion." In those days one had to become expert in dodging persons who were persuaded that the fourth dimension was the door to spiritualism, and the hasty evasion is not surprising. But those who quote and applaud the remark as though it were one of Einstein's most memorable utterances overlook a glaring fallacy in it. Natural selection is a purely scientific theory. If in the early days of Darwinism the then Archbishop had asked what effect the theory of natural selection would have on religion, ought the answer to have been "None. The Darwinian theory is a purely scientific theory, and has nothing to do with religion"?

The compartments into which human thought is divided are not so water-tight that fundamental progress in one is a matter of indifference to the rest. The great change in theoretical physics which began in the early years of the present century is a purely scientific development; but it must affect the general current of human thought, as at earlier times the Copernican and the Newtonian systems have done. This alone would seem to justify the scientific authors in taking a broad view of their task. It seems to me unreasonable to maintain that the working out of these wider implications of the new conception of the physical universe should be left entirely to those who do not understand it.

Not so very long ago the subject now called physics was known as "natural philosophy". The physicist is by origin a philosopher who has specialised in a particular direction. But he is not the only victim of specialisation. By the breaking away of physics the main body of philosophy suffered an amputation. In practice, if not in theory, academic philosophy has also become specialised, and is no longer co-extensive with the system of thought and knowledge by which we orient ourselves towards our moral and material environment. To a man's philosophy in the broadest sense—to his *religio vitae*—natural philosophy, under the name of science, has continued to be a powerful, perhaps even a predominant, contributor. It would be difficult to point to any development in academic philosophy which has had so great an influence on man's outlook as the growth of the scientific theory of evolution. In the last twenty years it has been the turn of physics to reassert itself as natural philosophy; and I believe that the new contribution of physical science, if fully grasped, is not less significant than the doctrine of evolution.

We may define rather more closely the status of a scientist

who writes on the philosophical outcome of modern physical theories. I do not think that any school of philosophers is prepared to wash its hands of the physical universe and leave the physicists to make what they like of it. It seems therefore to be agreed that scientific epistemology is still an integral part of philosophy. Those whose work lies in the epistemological developments of modern physics must therefore be counted as specialists in one of the departments into which philosophy is divided—a department not far from the heart of the subject. In their discussion of philosophy as a whole they are likely to display the faults of a specialist who finds himself outside his own groove; but they are not common intruders. The evils of specialisation would, I think, be still more pronounced if they made no attempt to correlate with the rest of philosophy the progress that has been made in their own department.

Scientific epistemology is the main theme of these lectures. We shall consider it primarily from the scientific aspect. But we shall also at times endeavour to view it in its general setting as a region of overlap of physics and philosophy, and trace its consequences in both fields.

IV

For the truth of the conclusions of physical science, observation is the supreme Court of Appeal. It does not follow that every item which we confidently accept as physical knowledge has actually been certified by the Court; our confidence is that it would be certified by the Court if it were submitted. But it does follow that every item of physical knowledge is of a form which might be submitted to the Court. It must be such that we can specify (although it may be impracticable to carry out) an observational procedure which would decide whether it is true or not. Clearly a statement cannot be tested by observation unless it is an assertion about the results of observation. *Every item of physical knowledge must therefore be an assertion of what has been or would be the result of carrying out a specified observational procedure.*

I do not think that anyone—least of all, those who are critical of the modern tendencies of physics—will disagree with the first axiom of scientific epistemology, namely that the knowledge obtained by the methods of physical science is limited to observational knowledge in the sense explained above. We do not deny that knowledge which is not of an observational nature may exist, e.g. the theory of numbers in pure mathematics; and non-committally we may allow the possibility of other forms of insight of the human mind into a world outside itself. But such knowledge is beyond the borders of physical science, and therefore does not enter into the description of the world introduced in the formulation of physical knowledge. To a wider synthesis of knowledge, of which physical knowledge is only a part, we may perhaps correlate a "world" of which the physical universe is only a partial aspect. But at this stage of our inquiry we limit the discussion to physical knowledge, and therefore to a physical universe from which, by definition, all characteristics which are not the subject of physical knowledge are excluded.

A distinction is commonly made between observational and theoretical knowledge; but in practice the terms are used so loosely as to deprive the classification of all real significance. The whole development of physical science has been a process of combining theory and observation; and in general every item of physical knowledge—or at least every item to which attention is ordinarily directed—has a partly observational and partly theoretical basis. The distinction, so far as it can be made, has reference to the mode of obtaining the knowledge—to the nature of the evidence for its truth. It does not concern the knowledge itself—what it is we intend to assert. Thus our axiom that all physical knowledge is of an observational nature is not to be understood as excluding theoretical knowledge. I *know* the position of Jupiter last night. That is knowledge of an observational nature; it is possible to detail the observational procedure which yields the quantities (right ascension and declination) which express my knowledge of the planet's position. As a matter of fact I did not follow this procedure, nor did I learn the position from anyone who had followed the procedure; I looked it up in the Nautical Almanac. That gave me the result of a computation according to planetary theory. Present-day physics accepts that theory and all its consequences; that is to say, it admits the calculated position as a foreknowledge of the results which would be obtained by carrying out the recognised observational procedure. Of my two pieces of knowledge, namely knowledge of the results of a mathematical computation and foreknowledge of the results of an observational procedure, it is the latter which I assert when I claim to know the position of Jupiter. If, on submission to the Court of Appeal, my foreknowledge of the result of the observational procedure proves to be incorrect, I shall have to admit that I was mistaken and did not know the position of Jupiter; it will be no use my urging that my knowledge of the result of the mathematical computation was correct.

It is the essence of acceptance of a theory that we agree to obliterate the distinction between knowledge derived from it and knowledge derived from actual observation. It may seem one-sided that the obliteration of the distinction should render all physical knowledge observational in nature. But not even the most extreme worshipper of theory has proposed the reverse—that in accepting the results of an observational research as trustworthy we elevate them to the status of theoretical conclusions. The one-sidedness is due to our acceptance of observation, not theory, as the supreme Court of Appeal.

V

We have seen that every item of physical knowledge, whether derived from observation or theory or from a combination of both, is an assertion of what has been or would be the result of carrying out a specified observational procedure. Generally it is an assertion of what *would be* the result if an observation were made; for this reason it is more accurate to describe physical knowledge as *hypothetico-observational.** Occasionally the hypothetical form can be dropped—the observation has been made and the result obtained—but the proportion of knowledge to which this applies is small, and mostly uninteresting. I am not denying the importance of actual observation as a source of knowledge; but as a constituent of scientific knowledge it is almost negligible. Whenever in the process of reducing observations a "correction" is applied, observational knowledge of an actual experiment is replaced by hypothetico-observational knowledge of what would have been the result of an experiment under more ideal conditions.

Consider, for example, our knowledge that the distance of the moon is about 240,000 miles. The exact meaning of this assertion must be ascertained by reference to the definition of distance in physics and astronomy (Chapter v); but, accurately enough for present purposes, what we claim to know is that 240,000 × 1760 yard-sticks placed end to end would reach from here to the moon. This is hypothetico-observational knowledge; for certainly no one has carried out the experiment. It is true that actual observations were employed in arriving at the figure 240,000 miles; but apart from theory we should not know that the resulting quantity was the distance of the moon. There are a variety of practical

* "Hypothetico-observational knowledge" means knowledge of the result of a hypothetical observation, not hypothetical interpretation of the result of an actual observation.

methods of finding the distance; one of the most accurate involves *inter alia* swinging pendulums in different latitudes on the earth. Although it would be true to assert that 240,000 miles is the result of an actual observational procedure of swinging pendulums, etc., that is not what we intend to assert when we say that the distance of the moon is 240,000 miles. By employing accepted theory we have been able to substitute for the actual observational procedure a hypothetical observational procedure which would yield the same result if it were carried out. The gain is that hypothetico-observational knowledge can be systematised and gathered into a coherent whole, whereas actual observational knowledge is sporadic and desultory.

One cannot help feeling a misgiving that hypothetico-observational knowledge is not entirely satisfactory from a logical standpoint. What exactly is the status of conditional knowledge if the condition is not fulfilled? Can any sense at all be attributed to a statement that if something, which we know did not happen, had happened, then certain other things would have happened? Yet I cannot help prizing my knowledge that $240,000 \times 1760$ yard-sticks *would* reach from here to the moon, although there is no prospect that they ever *will* do so.

VI

Scientific study of the facts of observation has led us to make a number of generalisations which we call laws of nature. Generalisation is the most conspicuous source of the hypothetico-observational character of physical knowledge, since it flagrantly oversteps actual observation and asserts knowledge of what would be observed on any occasion if the necessary procedure were carried out.

I think it is sometimes maintained that a law of nature is a systematisation, not a generalisation, of knowledge. Ideally it is possible to accept a systematisation of existing observational knowledge, without prejudging whether any future observations will conform to the system. To a person holding this view it should be a complete surprise every time a new observation is found to obey the law. For example, Bode's law of planetary distances can be regarded as a systematised statement concerning the distances of the six planets known in his time, and not expected to apply to planets discovered subsequently. This may be the right attitude to adopt towards particular laws that have been enunciated; but it certainly cannot be applied generally throughout physics. We must not imagine that Bode's systematisation would continue to be possible in a physics purged of generalisations. Unless we accept certain prior generalisations, e.g. that light travels in straight lines, the distances of the planets cannot be determined; and Bode's law then drops out, because there is no material for it to systematise. The fact is that generalisation from observation has, whether advertently or not, been practised in physical science from the very beginning; and we must regard it as no less part of the scientific method than observation itself. And with the generalisations there has entered into the body of scientific knowledge a hypothetico-observational element, which has been conceded the right to remain.

Our main conclusion is that, notwithstanding the diversity of method, physical knowledge remains homogeneous in its nature; it is knowledge of what would be the result of an observational procedure if it were carried out, including as a special case the result of any observational procedure that has been carried out.

In the progress of physics individual facts have become largely merged in generalisations. Would it be true to say that complete knowledge of physics would consist wholly of such generalisations? The answer is different according as we refer to physics in a narrow sense (including chemistry, but not astronomy or other observational, as distinguished from experimental, sciences) or to physical science generally. In the narrow sense physics is, I think, concerned solely with generalisations. The physicist is not interested in special facts except as material for generalisation. If he studies a particular lump of iron, it is as a sample exhibiting the general properties of iron. The astronomer on the other hand *is* interested in the particular lump of matter on which we happen to live, whether or not it is a sample of planets generally. He is curious about the existence of vegetation on Mars, when the next bright comet will appear, how closely a minor planet approached the earth, and so on. It may be said that this is just an amateurish interest which the more serious-minded physicist has outgrown; an astronomer must, of course, ascertain the constants of the earth, as a physicist must ascertain the constants of his galvanometer, but he has no business to be *interested* in them. Astronomers will scarcely agree; but let that pass. It is sufficient to say that these special facts are knowledge acquired by the methods of physical science, and must not be neglected in scientific epistemology which we have defined as the study of the nature of the knowledge that has come to us in this way; nor are they negligible in the universe of which that knowledge forms a description.

We must therefore remember that not all our knowledge of the physical universe is comprised in knowledge of the laws of nature. The warning is not so superfluous as it seems. I have often found an impression that to explain away the laws of nature as wholly subjective is the same thing as to explain away the physical universe as wholly subjective. Such a view is altogether unfounded.

CHAPTER II

SELECTIVE SUBJECTIVISM

I

LET us suppose that an ichthyologist is exploring the life of the ocean. He casts a net into the water and brings up a fishy assortment. Surveying his catch, he proceeds in the usual manner of a scientist to systematise what it reveals. He arrives at two generalisations:

(1) No sea-creature is less than two inches long.
(2) All sea-creatures have gills.

These are both true of his catch, and he assumes tentatively that they will remain true however often he repeats it.

In applying this analogy, the catch stands for the body of knowledge which constitutes physical science, and the net for the sensory and intellectual equipment which we use in obtaining it. The casting of the net corresponds to observation; for knowledge which has not been or could not be obtained by observation is not admitted into physical science.

An onlooker may object that the first generalisation is wrong. "There are plenty of sea-creatures under two inches long, only your net is not adapted to catch them." The ichthyologist dismisses this objection contemptuously. "Anything uncatchable by my net is *ipso facto* outside the scope of ichthyological knowledge, and is not part of the kingdom of fishes which has been defined as the theme of ichthyological knowledge. In short, what my net can't catch isn't fish." Or—to translate the analogy—"If you are not simply guessing, you are claiming a knowledge of the physical universe discovered in some other way than by the methods of physical science, and admittedly unverifiable by such methods. You are a metaphysician. Bah!"

The dispute arises, as many disputes do, because the protagonists are talking about different things. The onlooker has in mind an objective kingdom of fishes. The ichthyologist is not concerned as to whether the fishes he is talking about form an objective or subjective class; the property that matters is that they are catchable. His generalisation is perfectly true of the class of creatures he is talking about—a selected class perhaps, but he would not be interested in making generalisations about any other class. Dropping analogy, if we take observation as the basis of physical science, and insist that its assertions must be verifiable by observation, we impose a selective test on the knowledge which is admitted as physical. The selection is subjective, because it depends on the sensory and intellectual equipment which is our means of acquiring observational knowledge. It is to such subjectively-selected knowledge, and to the universe which it is formulated to describe, that the generalisations of physics— the so-called laws of nature—apply.

It is only with the recent development of epistemological methods in physics that we have come to realise the far-reaching effect of this subjective selection of its subject matter. We may at first, like the onlooker, be inclined to think that physics has missed its way, and has not reached the purely objective world which, we take it for granted, it was trying to describe. Its generalisations, if they refer to an objective world, are or may be rendered fallacious through the selection. But that amounts to condemning observationally grounded science as a failure because a purely objective world is not to be reached by observation.

Clearly an abandonment of the observational method of physical science is out of the question. Observationally grounded science has been by no means a failure; though we may have misunderstood the precise nature of its success. Those who are dissatisfied with anything but a purely objective universe may turn to the metaphysicians, who are not cramped by the self-imposed ordinance that every assertion must be capable of submission to observation as the final Court of Appeal. But we, as physicists, shall continue to study the universe revealed by observation and to make our generalisations about it; although we now know that the universe so reached cannot be wholly objective. Of course, the great mass of physicists, who pay no attention to epistemology, would have gone on doing this in any case.

Should we then ignore the onlooker with his suggestion of selection? I think not; though we cannot accept his remedy. Suppose that a more tactful onlooker makes a rather different suggestion: "I realise that you are right in refusing our friend's hypothesis of uncatchable fish, which cannot be verified by any tests you and I would consider valid. By keeping to your own method of study, you have reached a generalisation of the highest importance—to fishmongers, who would not be interested in generalisations about uncatchable fish. Since these generalisations are so important, I would like to help you. You arrived at your generalisation in the traditional way by examining the fish. May I point out that you could have arrived more easily at the same generalisation by examining the net and the method of using it?"

The first onlooker is a metaphysician who despises physics on account of its limitations; the second onlooker is an epistemologist who can help physics because of its limitations. It is just because of the limited—some might say, the perverted—aim of physics that such help is possible. The traditional method of systematic examination of the data furnished by observation is not the only way of reaching the generalisations valued in physical science. Some at least of these generalisations can also be found by examining the sensory and intellectual equipment used in observation. Epistemology thus presents physics with a new method of achieving its aims. The development of relativity theory, and the transformation of quantum theory from an empirical to a rational theory are the outcome of the new method; and in it is our great hope of further fundamental advances.

II

We return to our fish to illustrate another point of great importance. No suggestion was offered as to the second generalisation—that all sea-creatures have gills—and, so far as we can see, it could not have been deduced from an examination of the net and its mode of use. If the ichthyologist extends his investigations, making further catches, perhaps in different waters, he may any day bring up a sea-creature without gills and upset his second generalisation. If this happens, he will naturally begin to distrust the security of his first generalisation. His fear is needless; for the net can never bring up anything that it is not adapted to catch.

Generalisations that can be reached epistemologically have a security which is denied to those that can only be reached empirically.

It has been customary in scientific philosophy to insist that the laws of nature have no compulsory character; they are uniformities which have been found to occur hitherto in our limited experience, but we have no right to assert that they will occur invariably and universally. This was a very proper philosophy to adopt as regards empirical generalisations—it being understood, of course, that no one would be so foolish as to apply the philosophy in practice. Scientists, assured by their philosophy that they had no right to expectations, continued to cherish indefensible expectations, and interpreted their observations in accordance with them. Attempts have been made by the theory of probability to justify our expectation that if an occurrence (whose cause is unknown) has happened regularly hitherto it will continue to happen on the next occasion; but I think that all that has emerged is an analysis and axiomatisation of our expectation, not a defence of it.

The situation is changed when we recognise that some laws of nature may have an epistemological origin. These are compulsory; and when their epistemological origin is established, we have a right to our expectation that they will be obeyed invariably and universally. The process of observing, of which they are a consequence, is independent of time or place.

But, it may be objected, can we be sure that the process of observing* is unaffected by time or place? Strictly speaking, no. But if it is affected—if position in time and space or any other circumstance prevents the observational procedure from being carried out precisely according to the recognised specification—we can (and do) call the resulting observation a "bad observation". Those who resent the idea of compulsion in scientific law may perhaps be mollified by the concession that, although it can no longer be accepted as a principle of scientific philosophy that the laws of nature are uncompulsory, there is no compulsion that our actual observations shall satisfy them, for (unfortunately) there is no compulsion that our observations shall be *good* observations.

What about the remaining laws of nature, not of an epistemological origin, and therefore, so far as we know,

* The standard specification of the procedure of observing must be sufficiently detailed to secure a unique result of the observation. It is the duty of the observer to secure that all attendant circumstances which can affect the result, e.g., temperature, absence of magnetic field, etc., are in accordance with specification. Epistemological laws governing the results of the observation are such as are inferable solely from the fact that the procedure was as specified. The contingency referred to in this paragraph is exemplified by the fact that it is impossible to make a really "good" observation of length in a strong magnetic field, because the standard specification of the procedure of determining length requires us to eliminate magnetic fields (p. 80).

non-compulsory? Must they continue to mar the scheme as a source of indefensible expectations, which nevertheless are found to be fulfilled in practice? Before worrying about them, it will be well to wait till we see what is left of the system of natural law after the part which can be accounted for epistemologically has been removed. There may not be anything left to worry about.

The introduction of epistemological analysis in modern physical theory has not only been a powerful source of scientific progress, but has given a new kind of security to its conclusions. Or, I should rather say, it has put a new kind of security within reach. Whether the present conclusions are secure is a question of human fallibility, from which the epistemologist is no more exempt than the classical theorist or the practical observer. Whilst not forgetting that the actual results achieved must depend on the insight and accuracy of those who use the equipment, I would emphasise that we have now the equipment to put theoretical physics on a surer footing than it formerly aspired to.

III

Quis custodiet ipsos custodes? Who will observe the observers? The answer is—the epistemologist. He watches them to see what they really observe, which is often quite different from what they say they observe. He examines their procedure and the essential limitations of the equipment they bring to their task, and by so doing becomes aware beforehand of limitations to which the results they obtain will have to conform. They, on the other hand, only discover these limitations when they come to examine their results, and, unaware of their subjective origin, hail them as laws of nature.

It may be argued that, in accepting the aid of epistemology, physical science continues to be wholly an inference from observation; for the epistemologist too is an observer. The astronomer observes stars; the epistemologist observes observers. Both are seeking a knowledge which rests on observation.

I am sorry I must offend the observationalists by rejecting this sop to traditional views; but the analogy between observing stars and observing observers will not hold good. The common statement that physical science rests on observation, and that its generalisations are generalisations about observational data, is not quite the whole truth. It rests on *good* observation, and its generalisations are about *good* observational data. Scientific epistemology, which is concerned with the nature of the knowledge contained in physical science, has therefore to examine the procedure of good observation. The proper counterpart to the epistemologist who observes good observers is the astronomer who observes good stars.

This qualification of observations as "good", which is the first point attended to in practice, seems often to have been overlooked in philosophy. In speaking of observation, there is often a failure to distinguish the special kind of observational activity contemplated in physical science from indiscriminately "taking notice". The distinction is strongly selective; and it indicates one way in which the subjective selection, to which we have referred, is introduced into the universe described by physics. If astronomers were similarly allowed to distinguish good stars and bad stars, astronomy would doubtless be enriched by some remarkable new laws—applying, of course, only to the good stars which obey the laws so prescribed.

Whether an observation is good or bad depends on what it professes to represent. A bad determination of the melting-point of sulphur may be an excellent determination of the melting-point of a mixture of sulphur and dirt. The terms used to describe an observation—to state what it is an observation of—imply by their definition a standard procedure to be followed in making it; the observer professes to follow this procedure, or a procedure which he takes the liberty of substituting for it in the belief that it will assuredly give the same result. If, through inadvertence or practical difficulty, the prescribed conditions of the procedure are not carried out, the observation is a bad observation, and the observer in this instance is a bad observer. Equally from the point of view of physical science he is a bad observer if his belief that his method can be substituted for the standard procedure is mistaken; though in this case he will pass the blame on to the theorist who advised him wrongly.

The epistemologist accordingly does not study the observers as organisms whose activities must be ascertained empirically in the same way that a naturalist studies the habits of animals. He has to pick out the good observers—those whose activities follow a conventional plan of procedure. What the epistemologist must get at is this plan. Without it, he does not know which observers to study and which to ignore; with it, he need not actually watch the good observers who, he knows already, are merely following its instructions, since otherwise they would not be good.

The plan must be sought for in the mind of the observer, or in the minds of those from whom he has derived his instructions. The epistemologist is an observer only in the sense that he observes what is in the mind. But that is a pedantic description of the way in which we discover a plan conceived in anyone's mind. We learn the observer's plan by listening to his own account of it and cross-questioning him.

IV

We may distinguish knowledge of the physical universe derived by study of the results of observation as *a posteriori* knowledge, and knowledge derived by epistemological study of the procedure of observation as *a priori* knowledge. A valuer may arrive at the generalisation *a posteriori* that no article in a certain house is worth more than sixpence; the same generalisation might also have been reached *a priori* by noticing that the owner furnished it from Woolworth's. The observer is called upon to supply the furniture of the mansion of science. The priorist by watching his method of obtaining the furniture may anticipate some of the conclusions which the posteriorist will reach by inspecting the furniture.

I think that I am here using the term "*a priori* knowledge" with its recognised meaning—knowledge which we have of the physical universe prior to actual observation of it. At any rate epistemological knowledge is near enough akin to *a priori* knowledge to arouse the same opposition from physicists of the traditional school. *A priori* knowledge has disreputable associations in science; and I am not going to try to conceal the family skeleton by quibbling about names.

To be quite explicit—epistemological or *a priori* knowledge is prior to the carrying out of the observations, but not prior to the development of a plan of observation. As physical knowledge, it is necessarily an assertion of the results of observations imagined to be carried out. To the question whether it can be regarded as independent of observational experience altogether, we must, I think, answer no. A person without observational experience at all, and without that indirect knowledge of observational experience which he might gain by communication with his fellows, could not possibly attach meaning to the terms in which epistemological knowledge, like other physical knowledge, is expressed; and it would be impossible to put it into any other form which would have a meaning for him.

We must grant then that the deduction of a law of nature from epistemological considerations implies antecedent observational experience. But it must be emphasised that the relation of the law of nature to the observations which form this antecedent experience is altogether different from its relation to the observations which it governs. A stranger to our University, observing that undergraduates were inside their Colleges before midnight, might believe that he had discovered a law of human nature—that there is something in the nature of the undergraduate which impels him to seek the protection of the college walls before the stroke of twelve. We must undeceive him, and point out that the law has a quite different source—the College authorities. Should he conclude then that the law is altogether independent of undergraduate nature? Not necessarily. Careful research would reveal that the law depends on considerable antecedent experience of undergraduate nature. We cannot say that the twelve o'clock rule is not based on undergraduate nature; but it is not based on it in the way the stranger assumed.

In physical science *a priori* conclusions have long been anathema; and we must expect opposition from those who adhere to tradition. It has come to be accepted as a scientific principle that we can have no *a priori* knowledge of the universe. Agreed: provided that by "universe" is here meant "objective universe", as was undoubtedly intended when the principle was framed. But, as applied to a universe defined as the theme of physical knowledge rather than by its intrinsic characteristics,* the principle cancels itself. If we cannot have *a priori* knowledge of the universe, we cannot

* When we have defined a thing, we have *a priori* knowledge that it has the characteristics specified in the definition. The principle must evidently be understood to except this *a priori* knowledge.

have *a priori* knowledge that it is objective; and therefore we cannot have *a priori* knowledge that we cannot have *a priori* knowledge of it.

The re-introduction of *a priori* physical knowledge is justified by the discovery that the universe which physical science describes is partially subjective. Historically the argument is the other way about. It has been found that certain knowledge can be obtained by *a priori* methods; it is undoubtedly knowledge of the universe of physics, because it is precisely the knowledge which physicists have sought, and in some cases found, by the usual *a posteriori* methods. But, admittedly, such *a priori* knowledge would be impossible if the universe to which it relates were wholly objective. This starts us on an inquiry in which we are able to trace the mode of entry of a subjective element into the universe of physics.

It seems appropriate to call the philosophical outlook that we have here reached *selective subjectivism*. "Selective" is to be interpreted broadly. I do not wish to assert that the influence of the procedure of observing on the knowledge obtained is confined to simple selection, like passing through a net. But the term will serve to remind us that the subjective and the objective can be combined in other ways than by mere addition. In mathematics a very general type of such combination is that of operator and operand, selective operators being a particular case.

Selection implies something to select from. It seems permissible to conclude that the material on which the selection is performed is objective. The only way to satisfy ourselves of this is to examine carefully the ways in which subjectivity can creep into physical knowledge through the procedure of observing. So far as I can see, selection or operations mathematically akin to it cover the whole range of possibility; that is to say, the whole subjectivity is comprised in operations of a selective type. The subjectivity being confined to the operators, the ultimate operand must be free from subjectivity.

I see no reason to doubt the foregoing argument, but it depends on a vigilance of scrutiny which I cannot guarantee as conclusive. "Objective" is essentially a negative characteristic (non-subjective) of knowledge, although we regard it as a positive characteristic of the thing to which the knowledge refers; and it is always more difficult to demonstrate a negative than a positive conclusion. I accept an objective element in physical knowledge on, I think, reasonably strong grounds, but not with the same assurance as the subjective element which is easily demonstrable.

Selective subjectivism, which is the modern scientific philosophy, has little affinity with Berkeleian subjectivism, which, if I understand rightly, denies all objectivity to the external world. In our view the physical universe is neither wholly subjective nor wholly objective—nor a simple mixture of subjective and objective entities or attributes.

CHAPTER III

UNOBSERVABLES

I

THE fundamental ideas of modern physics, in so far as they differ from the classical ideas of the nineteenth century, are contained in two comprehensive theories—relativity theory and quantum theory. Relativity theory arrived in two stages, namely Einstein's special theory in 1905, and his general theory in 1915; to these should be added Weyl's theory of relativity of gauge in 1918, which is now an essential part of the relativistic conception. Quantum theory began in a paper by Planck in 1901; it is thus somewhat the older of the two theories, but it has been much longer in reaching maturity. Whereas relativity theory from the beginning was associated with a new philosophical outlook, quantum theory up to 1925 contributed nothing to philosophy except bewilderment. Heisenberg introduced an important new idea in 1925; and in the next year or two, through the aid of a number of contributors, the theory reached its present form, generally called "wave mechanics". It ceased to be entirely a collection of empirical magic; and, although still rather obscure, it contains certain coherent lines of thought which have philosophical implications not less important than those of relativity theory.

Two broad divisions of the subject matter of physics are recognised, namely *microscopic physics* which deals with systems on an atomic scale, and *molar physics* which deals with systems on a scale appreciable to our gross senses, comprising vast numbers of microscopic constituents. We generally say that relativity theory applies to molar systems and quantum theory to microscopic systems. That does not mean that Nature is divided against herself. In accepting relativity principles or quantum principles we accept them for the whole of physics; but they may have a more direct practical application to one branch than to the other. The quantum "principle of uncertainty" is presumably valid also for molar systems; but it would be difficult to produce a molar example in which the uncertainty is detectable. The "special principle of relativity", which asserts the primitive equivalence of the space-time frames corresponding to different velocities, is valid also in microscopic physics; but it has no direct application to the interior of an atom or of a nucleus since, as a reference frame for internal structure, a space-time frame in which the atom or nucleus as a whole is in motion is not equivalent to one in which it is at rest. Relativity and quantum *principles* are valid throughout physics; but the collections of theorems and formulae which are commonly said to constitute relativity theory and quantum theory, respectively, adhere fairly closely to the division between molar and microscopic physics.

The relation between the microscopic (quantum) laws of physics and the molar laws was made clear by Niels Bohr in his "correspondence principle". The molar laws are a simplified form to which the microscopic laws converge when the number of particles or quanta considered is very large. This means that ideally the microscopic laws alone are sufficient to cover the whole field of physics, the molar laws being merely a convenient adaptation of them to a special, but frequently occurring, problem. We have so often to deal with collections of very large numbers of particles that it is useful to have a statement in compact form of the outcome of the microscopic laws as applied to such systems, taking advantage of the simplifications which occur when averaging is permissible. Molar law is this condensed and bowdlerised version of microscopic law.

Accordingly, in a logical order of presentation, microscopic law should precede molar law. But practical experience has presented the problem the other way round, since our sensory organs are themselves molar systems. Thus scientific investigation came across the molar laws first; and these have been welded into a logically complete scheme in relativity theory. Microscopic theory is intrinsically more difficult, and has had a later start; few of the more significant phenomena associated with quantum theory were known before 1900. In a survey of physical knowledge at the present epoch, it is impossible to avoid giving molar law an adventitious prominence (which will presumably not be permanent), since we are acquainted with a complete system of molar laws, but are still painfully trying to perfect the partially unravelled scheme of microscopic laws.

A study of mob-psychology would be a very unsatisfactory foundation for a theory of the human mind. The molar law, or mob-law, of physics is an equally unsatisfactory introduction to the theory of individual or atomic behaviour. Thus no sooner had we seemed to reach a comprehension of the ways of Nature in molar law than an entirely new conception of what she is about began to appear in microscopic law. Let me say at once that the analogy of the individual and the mob is imperfect. It is one of the interesting features of our progress that we have found it to be imperfect. This is because the individual particle or entity in physics is a much more elusive conception than the older atomists realised. But it remains true that much that is vital to a proper understanding of the physical universe is ordinarily lost to observation through the excessive smoothing effect of our gross senses; and the very pattern of natural law proves to be different from the conception we had formed from our first acquaintance with it in its limiting form for large numbers.

II

We frequently speak of "the principle of relativity"; but it is difficult to find a rigorous and authoritative enunciation of the principle. I have published three fairly long expositions of relativity, but, if my memory does not deceive me, none of them attempts a *definition* of the general principle of relativity.★ I think others have been equally reticent. For my own part I have regarded relativity as a new outlook whose consequences must gradually unfold themselves, rather than as a particular axiom or hypothesis to be translated once for all into definite formulation.

Perhaps the nearest approach to a formulation of the principle is the statement that we observe only *relations* between physical entities. This requires a certain amount of critical explanation which I shall not enter on now. For, as I have said, I would rather identify relativity with the outlook which leads to this conclusion. I would emphasise the question "What is it we really observe?" rather than the answer "We only observe relations between physical entities". Because as soon as we ask the question, the classical scheme of physics is a punctured bubble; and we start on a path of revolution of which perhaps the end is not yet in sight. It is common to describe the state of theoretical physics in the last thirty years as a succession of revolutions; but it is all one revolutionary movement which was started by this simple question. Heisenberg repeated the question in 1925: "What is it we really observe in an atom?" The result was the new quantum mechanics.

Our first epistemological conclusion was that physical knowledge is of an observational nature, in the sense that each item is an assertion of the result of an observation, actual or hypothetical. Clearly the next step must be to inquire

★ The "special" principle is a comparatively simple idea.

precisely what is comprised in the term "observation". The observer of observers—the epistemologist—must set to work to find out what observation really assures us of. In raising the question "What is it we really observe?" relativity theory summoned epistemology to the aid of science.

This second step is so comprehensive that it must be taken in stages. At each stage we reach only a partial truth; but, after the manner of science, we are more concerned to appreciate and develop the new insight revealed to us in the partial truth than to strive prematurely after a final answer. Progress so far has consisted, not so much in specifying what is actually observed, as in eliminating what is definitely unobserved and unobservable. Accordingly in this chapter we shall consider especially the situation created by the discovery that certain quantities, prominent in pre-relativity physics, are "unobservables".

As detective-story writers are fond of pointing out, it is notoriously difficult to extract from a witness the actual evidential facts; he cannot help wrapping them up in a gloss of his own. The habit of rough and ready inference comes to us early by instinct or education; and the "plain man of science" mixes his facts with crude and unreliable inferences, like any other witness, when he has to state what he has observed. Relativity theory made the first serious attempt to insist on dealing with the facts themselves. Previously scientists professed profound respect for the "hard facts of observation"; but it had not occurred to them to ascertain what they were.

Dividing physicists into three classes—relativity physicists, quantum physicists, experimental physicists—the relativity physicist studies the hard facts of observation. The quantum physicist follows the same principle as far as he can; but owing to the more intricate and more remote nature of his subject, the aim of constructing a theory which shall embrace only the observable facts represents his ideal rather than his achievement. As for the experimental physicist, I will only say that because a man works in a laboratory it does not follow that he is not an incorrigible metaphysician.

III

I will begin the discussion of unobservables by reminding you that the detection of even a single unobservable, which has gate-crashed into physical knowledge, may have far-reaching consequences. The foundation of the special theory of relativity, and the beginning of the modern revolution in physics, was the realisation that "velocity of the aether" is unobservable. If we say that the moon is distant 240,000 miles, we are asserting what would be the result of a certain observational procedure if it were carried out; but if we say that in a certain region the aether has a velocity of 80 km. per sec. relative to the earth, we are not asserting the result of any observational procedure, actual or hypothetical.

Let me first remove a common misunderstanding. I do *not* mean that the ingenuity of experimental physicists has as yet been insufficient to devise an observational procedure which will measure the velocity of the aether. It is never the task of the experimenter to devise the observational procedure which is the *ultimate* test of the truth of a scientific assertion. That must be indicated unambiguously in the assertion itself, having regard to the definitions of the terms employed in it; otherwise it is incapable of submission to the Court of Appeal, and is inadmissible as an item of physical knowledge. Where the ingenuity of the experimenter is often required is in devising a procedure equivalent to, but more practicable than, the procedure referred to in the assertion. The discovery, which became the foundation of the special theory of relativity, was that the assertion that the aether has a relative velocity of 80 km. per sec. turns out on scrutiny not to specify any observational procedure at all.* The ingenuity of the experimenter is not called upon; for he cannot be asked to devise a practicable procedure equivalent to a procedure which has never been specified.

If we shut our eyes to the logical incoherency in the definition of aether velocity, it is possible to treat its unobservability as an ordinary physical hypothesis, suggested and confirmed by observation so far as it has yet been possible to test its consequences. Since aether is not matter, it cannot be assumed *a priori* that the usual attributes of matter—density, rigidity, momentum, etc.—are also attributes of the aether. Accordingly the hypothesis to be tested is that velocity, although a well-known attribute of matter, is not one of the attributes of the aether. Put in this way, it is not a truth that could have been foreseen *a priori*; it is a mildly surprising, but clearly possible, conclusion deduced *a posteriori* from the null result of experiments designed to detect effects which would be expected if there existed a luminiferous aether with the type of structure to which velocity could be attributed.

This attitude is popular with those who dislike the epistemological inquiry associated with the new developments of physics. It is so easy to cut short an argument one does not want to understand by saying: "I am not interested in your reasons, but I am quite willing to try any conclusion you may have reached as a hypothesis to be tested by observation. Then, if it is confirmed, it will take rank with the other confirmed hypotheses of physics, and we shall not need your arguments." By this kind of short-circuiting, the more difficult considerations are cut out of the subject; and we can embark at once on the straightforward mathematical deduction of the consequences of the hypothesis with a view

---

* On the understanding that the "aether" referred to is Maxwell's electromagnetic aether, defined as having the properties specified by Maxwell's equations.

to observational test. Thus the new wine is put into the old
bottles. It does not burst the bottles; but it loses most of its
invigorating—my opponents would perhaps say, its intoxi-
cating—qualities.

Let us try to recapture the invigoration. We can at least
see that the detection, whether by logical scrutiny or by
experimental test, of one unobservable masquerading as an
observable in the classical scheme of physics, and the important consequences which have resulted from the detection
should be followed up by a systematic search for other im-
postors. Several others have been found—in each case with
very far-reaching results. The best known is Heisenberg's
discovery that a combination of exact position with exact
velocity is not observable; this constitutes the famous
"uncertainty principle".

As a further example, it was pointed out ten years ago that
when we are dealing with particles, such as electrons, which
are indistinguishable from one another observationally, the
ordinary co-ordinate $\xi = x_2 - x_1$ of one particle relative to
another is not an observable; the observable in this case is a
type of quantity previously unfamiliar in analysis, namely a
"signless co-ordinate" $\eta = \pm\xi$. Up to the present, quantum
physicists have chosen to ignore this imposture; and the
modern text-books still adhere to the erroneous theory of
a system of two such particles, which assumes the observable
to be ξ. They have thereby missed the opening for a much
needed advance.

I have mentioned this last example because it is a clear
case in which unobservability is a matter of epistemological
principle, not of physical hypothesis. For simplicity, consider
particles in one dimension only, say east and west. If we
have a green ball and a red ball, we can observe that the
green ball is, say, 5 inches west of the red ball. Accordingly,
for purposes of description, we introduce an observable
quantity ξ which states the distance of the green ball from the

red ball measured towards the west; a negative value of ξ will indicate that the green ball is to the east. But suppose instead that we have two balls exactly alike in colour, and with no distinction at all that we can observe. In such a system there is no observable corresponding to ξ. We can observe that the balls are 5 inches apart in the east-west line, and we can introduce an observable η which states the distance apart. But, unlike ξ, η is a signless quantity.

It is a natural mistake to apply the ordinary theory of the observable behaviour of particles (*particle mechanics*, as we call it) to protons and electrons, overlooking that at an early stage in that theory, namely in introducing and defining a relative co-ordinate ξ, it was taken for granted that the particles could be distinguished observationally. This mechanics becomes inapplicable when ξ is unobservable. For protons and electrons we have a modified mechanics with η as the observable. This fundamental difference in the mechanics must be followed up mathematically; and although the problem is rather difficult, I think it is rigorously deducible that the difference is equivalent to a force between the particles which is actually the well-known Coulomb force. That is to say, the electrostatic (Coulomb) force between electrons and protons is not an "extra" arising we know not why, but is simply a term which had dropped out in the ordinary derivation of the equations through the oversight of taking ξ instead of η as the observable, and had therefore to be re-inserted empirically.

Those unfamiliar with wave-mechanics may be astonished that there should be a difference between the mechanics of distinguishable particles and the mechanics of indistinguishable particles. But it ought not to surprise quantum physicists, since it is universally admitted that there is a difference in their statistics, which is no less mysterious. Indeed I have never been able to understand why those who are well aware of the important consequences of indistinguishability in large assemblies do not trouble to examine its precise consequences in smaller systems. Whether we consider the well-known effect on the statistics of large assemblies or the less well-known effect on the mechanics of a system of two particles, the conclusions appear incredible unless we bear in mind the subjectivity of the world described by physics and of all that it is said to contain. It is naturally objected that the particles cannot be affected by our inability to distinguish them, and it is absurd to suppose that they modify their behaviour on that account. That would be true if we were referring to wholly objective particles and wholly objective behaviour. But our generalisations about their behaviour—the laws of mechanics—describe properties imposed by our procedure of observation, as the generalisations about catchable fish were imposed by the structure of the net. The objective particles are unconcerned with our inability to distinguish them; but they are equally unconcerned with the behaviour which we attribute to them partly as a consequence of our failure to distinguish them. It is this observable behaviour, and not the objective behaviour, that *we* are concerned with.

Returning to the question of physical hypothesis *versus* epistemological principle, it is conceivable that a man, unwilling to apply his mind to anything except mathematical formulae, might treat our assertion that the observable is η, not ξ, as a suggested hypothesis which must stand or fall by a comparison of the deduced consequences with experiment. In form it resembles a physical hypothesis, and its consequences can be followed up in the same way. But in this case the observational test is perfunctory—like the experimental verification of propositions of Euclid. A discordance might point to an error in deducing the observational consequences of the assertion, or it might signify that electrons are after all not entirely indistinguishable; but it would not persuade us to contradict ourselves by asserting that, when

A is observationally indistinguishable from *B*, it is possible to observe that *A* is to the west, not east, of *B*.

It would be an exaggeration to say that the unobservability of aether velocity is equally obvious epistemologically —that the impossibility of observing it leaps to the eye as soon as we consider how we should set about the observation. That is because reference to the aether involves us in a maze of half-forgotten definitions through which it is difficult to thread our way without losing ourselves in a dust-storm of verbal controversy. But the aether has few friends nowadays, and we attach more importance to a closely related unobservable, namely "distant simultaneity". The unobservability of distant simultaneity is essentially the same principle as the unobservability of aether velocity, but it is free from the possibly ambiguous phraseology associated with the old aether hypotheses. The unobservability of distant simultaneity is found to be a purely epistemological conclusion.

The classical outlook took it for granted that, in the history of a body anywhere in space, there must occur an instant identified in an absolute way with the instant "now" which we ourselves are this moment experiencing. It was also taken for granted that the procedure, necessary to decide observationally which instants have this relation of absolute simultaneity, would be obvious to commonsense. But if simultaneity at distant places is to be employed as a scientific term, we cannot tolerate vagueness of definition, and must insist on precise instructions as to the observational procedure intended. It is found that attempts to formulate the instructions always end in a vicious circle. For example, the instruction may be to correlate instants at different places by light signals or radio signals, making correction for the time of transit; but when we inquire how we are to determine the latter correction, the instructions are to measure the time of transit with clocks *already* adjusted to show simultaneity. It does not require a Michelson-Morley experiment to prove to us that there is a vicious circle in this definition—though it is probable that the flaw would have long continued to escape our notice if the result of the Michelson-Morley experiment had not instigated a scrutiny.

The hint that a quantity is possibly an unobservable has sometimes been given by observation; that is to say, when attempts were made to measure it, it proved to be unexpectedly elusive. But our definite knowledge that it is unobservable does not come from the failure of attempts to observe it; it comes from a scrutiny of its definition, which is found to contain a self-contradiction or vicious circle or other logical flaw. The definition specifies something which sounds like an observational procedure; but when we examine the meaning of the terms (which often involves tracing a long chain of definitions), we find that the specification does not make sense. Since the discrimination of unobservables depends on a study of the procedure of obtaining observational knowledge, or alleged observational knowledge, and not on a study of the results of carrying out the procedure, it comes under scientific epistemology; and a principle of unobservability, such as the special relativity principle, the uncertainty principle, or the modified mechanics of indistinguishable particles, is an epistemological principle. Such principles have an altogether different status from physical hypotheses, though they lead to the same kind of practical consequences.

When an unobservable is introduced into a statement which professes to be an expression of physical knowledge, the statement is usually rendered meaningless; as an item of physical knowledge it must assert the result of a specified observational procedure, and the intrusion of a term which is without observational meaning causes a hiatus in the specification. But exceptionally it may happen that the unobservable is involved in such a way that the truth of the statement is independent of the value ascribed to it. It then does not vitiate the statement; because, although part of the observational instructions proves illusory, it does not really matter what result we suppose this part of the procedure to have given. For example, it is an item of physical knowledge that a body which has been moved four yards to the north and then three yards to the east will be five yards from the starting point. This applies to measurements on other planets besides the earth. Reasonably interpreted, it applies even on a non-rotating planet, although "north" is then an unobservable; for although the terms "north" and "east" are used in expressing the knowledge, its truth is independent of the result of the observational procedure by which the first of these two rectangular directions is laid down.

Thus there are two ways of dealing with the unobservables which have been inadvertently admitted in classical physics. One way is to reformulate our knowledge in such a way as to root them out altogether. The other way is to sterilise them; they can be allowed to remain provided that the assertions which contain reference to them remain true whatever value we ascribe to them—whatever result we suppose the illusory observational procedure to have given. Although cumbrous from a philosophical standpoint, the latter method is generally the most convenient in the practical development of physical science. It involves less interference with the traditional form of expression of our knowledge. We can more easily trace the consequences of the unobservability. The possible assertions which involve reference to unobservables are very much restricted in form, because they must possess an "invariance" which keeps them true however we change the supposed value of the unobservable. Ordinarily such a restriction would amount to a physical hypothesis—a hypothesis that the actual behaviour of things is in accordance with the restriction. But in the present case the restriction is at root a tautology; for it would be quite meaningless to make an assertion which did not conform to the restriction.

IV

The reader may have noticed that the examples we have given of the application of epistemological considerations to physics are not quite what he was led to expect in Chapter II. We there contemplated generalisations (laws of nature) arising from the selective effect of the procedure of observation. Here our examination of the procedure appears to have led to a different kind of discovery, namely that certain quantities incorporated in the current scheme of physics are unobservable. By developing the consequences of this unobservability, we can deduce laws of nature which had previously been discovered or suggested empirically, and thereby transfer them from an *a posteriori* to an *a priori* basis; but there is seemingly little as yet to support the outlook which I have called selective subjectivism.* I will try to show later that the divergence is only apparent. Meanwhile it may be noted that an apparent divergence was to be expected; because the philosophical inquiry in Chapter II approached the subject from the standpoint of observability, and the scientific inquiry in this chapter has approached it from the standpoint of unobservability, so that there is some way to travel before they meet.

Unobservability of a quantity arises from a logical contradiction in the definition which professes to specify the procedure for observing it. I must emphasize that this is not a question of captious criticism of the wording of the old definitions generally quoted as authoritative. We do not condemn a quantity as unobservable, until every effort has been made, by re-wording the definition if necessary, to remove contradictions. To make it clear that the criticism

---

* A hint in this direction was, however, noticed on p. 37.

is not merely verbal, I will refer again to the two unobservables that we have already discussed.

Take first the unobservability of the co-ordinate-difference
ξ of two indistinguishable particles. Here there is no question
of amending the definition of ξ; for it is indispensable in its
present form in the study of distinguishable particles. The
logical contradiction arises in applying it to indistinguishable
particles, overlooking that it presupposes the particles to be
distinguishable observationally.

The unobservability of distant simultaneity raises more
difficult considerations, because the concept has existed from
time immemorial, and it has been taken for granted that the
practical observer would know how to determine it without
precise instructions. On trying to formulate the precise
instructions, we have found that they contain a vicious
circle, presupposing a knowledge of something which in
turn presupposes a knowledge of distant simultaneity. But
we have to meet the objection that the instructions which we
(the relativists) knock down are those which we have ourselves drawn up; and if the instructions had been drawn up
by more sensible people, they would not have contained the
vicious circle. Our reply is that the more sensible people
have now had thirty years in which to come forward; but
no one has produced instructions free from a vicious circle.
We are willing to take reasonable trouble to find out a
meaning, however imperfectly expressed; but it is not mere
captiousness if we refuse to hold up the progress of physics
by endless search for a meaning where there is no reason to
suppose that a meaning exists.

As a matter of fact the pathetic faith of those who talked
about distant simultaneity that someone might one day be
clever enough to find out what they meant, has come rather
near to being justified. In cosmological investigations it has
been found that if the distribution of the galaxies throughout
space is uniform (or nearly uniform) there is a natural system

(or approximate system) of time-reckoning appropriate to the universe as a whole. The world-wide instants in this reckoning may reasonably be taken to define a distant simultaneity. But it would be far-fetched to identify this with the distant simultaneity referred to in the Newtonian system of physics. I do not believe that the classical physicist, in his references to simultaneity, had a premonition of a relation contingent on the existence and law of distribution of milliards of galaxies, unsuspected in the cosmology of his time.

V

A feature of the advance of theoretical physics has been a progressive diminution in the number of its fundamental hypotheses.

Although we commonly distinguish between *fundamental* physical hypotheses and *casual* hypotheses made to explain particular phenomena or to fill gaps in our observational knowledge of the objects around us, it is difficult to formulate a rigorous distinction. However, doubt seldom arises in practice; and without endorsing the current classification (which I shall later propose to replace by a more significant one) I use it as a classification which is recognised *de facto*. In the domain thus set apart we find the same ground being covered by a continually diminishing number of hypotheses.

The diminution has come about in a number of ways. Firstly, the abandonment of the ideal of a mechanical explanation of everything has eliminated a great deal of idle hypothesis. The properties of the fundamental entities of physics are now stated in the form of mathematical equations, instead of being "explained" by hypothetical mechanisms. Mathematical formulation is very economic of hypothesis. Subject to a certain reservation, it enables us to state a conclusion which does not go beyond the ascertained facts; it is no more than a systematised statement of what is observed.

The reservation is that, whereas the ascertained facts justify the mathematical formula within a limited degree of approximation, under limited conditions, and in a limited number of instances, the mathematical formula omits reference to these limitations. If we had to append to the formula a schedule of the instances in which it had been found to be true, its usefulness would evaporate. In one sense Einstein's (or Newton's) law of gravitation is not a hypothesis; it is a summary statement of what we have observed, within certain limits of approximation. It becomes a hypothesis when we assert that it is exact and universal. Since mathematical formulation is now adopted throughout the fundamental part of physics, the only fundamental hypotheses required are hypotheses of generalisation in this sense.

Another powerful factor in reducing the number of hypotheses has been the growing unification of physics. Branches, formerly treated independently, have been united; and it has been found that their separate sets of hypotheses were an unnecessary duplication. A notable example is the identification of light with electromagnetic waves, which eliminated at one stroke all the hypotheses of optics, the hypotheses of electromagnetism being adequate to cover the whole subject. Even if we count the identification of light with electromagnetic waves as a new physical hypothesis, the substitution of this sole hypothesis for the speculative aether theories of the nineteenth century is a substantial reduction. But the identity of light with electromagnetic waves cannot be counted as an internal hypothesis of physics, since it is altogether outside the province of physics to consider how the stimulation of the optic nerve by electromagnetic waves awakens in consciousness the sensation called light.

This elimination of hypothesis had made considerable progress before the introduction of epistemological methods.

It has always been the aim of scientific inquiry to trace a common cause underlying diverse phenomena; and the normal progress of physics has been towards a unification which will exhibit the whole ordering of the universe as the result of a few simple causes. We may compare it with geometry which reduces a great variety of theorems to a few elementary axioms. If the analogy with geometry were to hold good, there would be a limit to the elimination of hypothesis, for a geometry without any axioms at all is unthinkable. But an equally possible analogy is with the theory of numbers. There we have also a great variety of theorems, disclosing properties of numbers quite unforseeable to ordinary intelligence; and yet throughout the whole subject there is nothing that can be called an axiom. We shall find reason to believe that this is in closer analogy with the system of fundamental laws of physics.

With the coming of relativity theory yet a third method of reducing the number of hypotheses crept in, namely the replacement of physical hypotheses by epistemological principles. We have already noticed the way in which an epistemological conclusion can play the same part as a physical hypothesis so far as observational consequences are concerned.

We have seen (p. 20) that laws and properties which have an epistemological origin are compulsory and universal. It may be added that, in some cases at least, they are exact. For the unobservability of certain quantities—which is the most common form of statement of an epistemological principle—is traced to a logical contradiction in their definitions; and the consequences (in so far as they are reached by logical deduction alone, and not by combination with more or less uncertain and inexact hypotheses) are quite definite. The pervasion of fundamental physics by epistemology has therefore greatly changed its character, and brought exactitude within reach. So long as the methods were wholly *a posteriori*, there was no warrant for regarding the deduced laws of nature as better than approximations.

To avoid misapprehension it is best to state here (prematurely) that although we now recognise laws which we can confidently assert are exact, the subject-matter of these exact laws is probability. There is therefore not a corresponding precision in the laws of observational phenomena (as distinguished from the laws of *probability* of the phenomena); and, notwithstanding its newly acquired exactness, the system of fundamental physical laws is indeterministic.

VI

We have seen that in the modern theories of physics epistemological results perform part of the duty which was formerly allotted to physical hypotheses—which indeed is still often ascribed to physical hypotheses by those who do not look far enough into its origin. But it is not easy to give a straightforward example of a hypothesis of the older physics which has disappeared through this replacement. This is because the scheme of theoretical physics is very much interlocked. A single hypothesis is not meant to stand by itself; it presupposes that other hypotheses in the scheme have been accepted. Newton's law of gravitation does not account for the orbits of the planets or the fall of an apple unless his laws of motion are also accepted. Thus we cannot expect a one-to-one correspondence between physical hypotheses in the old physics and epistemological principles in the new scheme. An epistemological principle, such as the special principle of relativity, cuts athwart the whole scheme of hypothesis. The hypotheses required to supplement it are less extensive than the system of hypotheses previously accepted; but the change is not a simple omission of one or more hypotheses leaving the rest intact.

The best I can do is to make a comparison of the hypothetical elements in Newton's and Einstein's laws of gravitation. To facilitate comparison I divide Newton's hypothesis into three steps of increasing specialisation:

($1h$) There is a universal law of gravitation.
($2h$) It is expressible by a differential equation of the second order.
($3h$) The second order equation (in empty space) is $\nabla^2 \phi = 0$.

I may repeat that the hypothetical element is the generality and exactness of these statements. If we have in mind a certain limited degree of generality and accuracy, we may substitute "empirical truth" for "hypothesis" in ($2h$) and ($3h$).

Analysing Einstein's law similarly, we have:

($1e$) There is a universal law of gravitation.
($2h$) It is expressible by a differential equation of the second order.
($3e$) The second order equation (in empty space) is $G_{\mu\nu} = \lambda g_{\mu\nu}$.

The first and third steps, marked e (epistemological) are rigorously deducible from an examination of the observational procedure followed in obtaining the measurements which are deemed to establish the law of gravitation. They involve no physical hypothesis at all. But the third step is left suspended in the air until the second step is taken, and for this we still appeal to physical hypothesis. We must therefore take as a measure of the reduction of hypothesis the elimination of ($1h$) and ($3h$), leaving ($2h$) unchanged. But to this must be added a further reduction of hypothesis connected with the laws of motion. In Newtonian physics the laws of motion are additional hypotheses; but in the relativity scheme they are deducible as mathematical consequences of Einstein's law of gravitation.

I have little doubt that the step ($2h$) can also be traced to an epistemological origin; but to investigate this it is necessary to enlarge the scope of the discussion so as to cover virtually the whole of extra-nuclear physics, and not merely mechanics. This would merge the inquiry in the general problem of estimating how much hypothesis remains in the fundamental laws of physics after the epistemological purge has been carried out in its entirety. This will be considered in Chapter IV.

THE SCOPE OF EPISTEMOLOGICAL
METHOD

I

A LARGE part of the domain of physical science is adequately covered by classical physics. Usually the more recent advances are grafted on to this older knowledge, and appear as corrections to it. We have seen in the last chapter that epistemological scrutiny has revealed impostures and exposed logical fallacies in the definitions of quantities in the classical scheme. By presenting the results in this way, we show epistemology in a rather negative aspect—advancing physics by removing errors which were blocking its path.

Although a comparison with classical physics is the simplest, and generally the most useful, way of exhibiting the new advances, we should also endeavour to grasp the positive aspect of epistemologically grounded theory as a self-contained development of physics, which, if pursued from the beginning, will be unimpeded by the type of error that we have been considering.

Regarded in this way, the characteristic of epistemological physics is that it directly investigates *knowledge*, whereas classical physics investigated or endeavoured to investigate an *entity* (the external world) which the knowledge is said to describe. Accordingly the modern physicist has devised a technique appropriate to the investigation of knowledge of the kind admitted in physics; whereas the classical physicist devised a technique appropriate to the investigation of an entity such as he conceived the external world to be. If from the beginning we realise that it is observational knowledge that is being analysed—that the mathematical symbols represent elements of knowledge, not entities of the external world—unobservables cannot be introduced except by deliberate intent as auxiliary quantities in the mathematics. The modern physicist is often reproached for assuming that because he has no knowledge of a thing it is non-existent. But this is a misconception; there is no need to make *any* assumption about things of which we have no knowledge direct or indirect, since they cannot appear in an analysis of our knowledge.

This difference is most strikingly exhibited in modern quantum theory. According to the classical conception of microscopic physics, our task was to discover a system of equations which connects the positions, motions, etc. of the particles at one instant, with the positions, motions, etc. at a later instant. This problem has proved altogether baffling; we have no reason to believe that any determinate solution exists, and the search has been frankly abandoned. Modern quantum theory has substituted another task, namely to discover the equations which connect knowledge of the positions, motions, etc. at one instant with knowledge of the positions, motions, etc. at a later instant. The solution of this problem appears to be well within our power.

The mathematical symbolism describes our knowledge, and the mathematical equations trace the change of this knowledge with time. Our knowledge of physical quantities is always more or less inexact; but the theory of probability enables us to give an exact specification of inexact knowledge, including a specification of its inexactitude. The introduction of probability into physical theories emphasises the fact that it is knowledge that is being treated. For probability is an attribute of our knowledge of an event; it does not belong to the event itself, which must certainly occur or not occur.

Wave mechanics investigates the way in which probability redistributes itself as time elapses; it analyses it into waves and determines the laws of propagation of those waves. Generally the waves tend to diffuse; that is to say, our knowledge of the position (or of any other characteristic) of a system becomes vaguer the longer the time elapsed since an observation was made. A sudden accession to knowledge—our becoming aware of the result of a new observation—is a discontinuity in the "world" of probability-waves; the probability is reconcentrated, and the propagation starts again from the new distribution. There are exceptional forms of probability distribution of certain of the attributes of microscopic systems which do not diffuse, or diffuse very slowly; so that our knowledge of these attributes does not so rapidly grow out of date. Particular attention is lavished on these "steady states" and on the equations determining them, since they provide a basis for long-range predictions.

The statement often made, that in modern theory the electron is not a particle but a wave, is misleading. The "wave" represents our knowledge of the electron. The statement is, however, an inexact way of emphasising that the knowledge, not the entity itself, is the direct object of our study; and it may perhaps be excused by the fact that the terminology of quantum theory is now in such utter confusion that it is well-nigh impossible to make clear statements in it. The term "electron" has at least three different meanings* in common use in quantum theory, in addition to its loose application to the probability wave itself.

Wave mechanics shows us immediately why the distinction between observables and unobservables is so essential. A "good" observation of a quantity, although it does not determine the quantity precisely, narrows down the range in which it is likely to lie. It creates a condensation in the probability distribution of the quantity or, as we usually say, forms a wave packet in it. The method of wave mechanics

---

* Namely, the particle represented by a Dirac wave-function, the particle introduced in second quantisation and the particle represented by the internal (relative) wave-function of a hydrogen atom.

is to investigate the wave equations which govern the propagation of waves from such a source. But if the quantity is unobservable, these wave packets cannot be formed. A study of the propagation of waves which there is no means of producing can have no application to physics; and a theory which professes to deduce observationally verifiable results by such analysis is evidently vitiated by a mis-identification.

II

I expect I shall be accused of exaggerating the epistemo-logical element in modern physical theory, and before going farther I will try to examine this criticism.

From the time of Newton until recently the epistemology of science was stationary; for two hundred years the extension and ordering of our knowledge of the physical universe continued without modifying it. We have seen that the physicist is by origin a philosopher who has specialised in a particular direction; but for him epistemology had become ancient history, and he had long ceased to concern himself with it. Generally he prided himself on being a plain matter-of-fact person—which was his way of describing a man who accepted the naïve realism of Newtonian epistemology. If he indulged in philosophy at all, it was as a hobby kept apart from the serious occupation of advancing science.

Thus although scientific epistemology has always been part of the domain of physics, the physicist had left it so long uncultivated that, when at last he turned attention to it, his right-of-way was questioned. The re-entry into this neglected field was the beginning of the modern revolution of physics, the first result being the theory of relativity. But we must not look upon epistemology as a long-estranged relative who has unexpectedly bequeathed us a fortune in the principle of relativity. The sensible way to treat a rich relative is to invite him to rejoin the family circle, so that you can touch him for a lot more.

The question may be raised, How far does general opinion among leading physicists to-day recognise this reunion? It is difficult to ascertain. My impression is that the general attitude might be described as *grudging acceptance*. Appeal to new epistemological considerations may be allowed in emergency, but it is not permitted to become part of the routine of scientific advance. There is a general recognition that important advances have resulted from critical examination of the nature of our observational knowledge. I think too that the leading authorities would agree with my brief account of the method of quantum theory in the last section —that it proceeds by a direct analysis of knowledge of a system, instead of by an analysis of the system itself—and they would acknowledge that this change of method is responsible for all recent progress. They seem to be aware of the epistemological element introduced in the revolution of physics; and they have experience of the practical value of a rational epistemological outlook. But there is an unaccountable reluctance to develop scientific epistemology systematically. Although particular principles have secured recognition and are indeed worked to death, there seems to be no realisation that it would be profitable thoroughly to explore the epistemological method so as to develop it to the utmost advantage.

There are many new problems connected with the nucleus, radiation, cosmology, etc., which it is admitted that the present quantum theory cannot cover without some fundamental advance. One would have thought that we had learnt by now how to set about escape from this deadlock. Another appeal should be made to our rich relation epistemology who has rescued us on former occasions; another step forward should be taken in answering the fundamental question, What do we really observe? This way of advance is still open; we had halted only because the flood of new insight revealed by the earlier steps was for the moment more than we could bear. Whatever my own scientific work in this direction may signify, it at least shows where the openings lie, and that advance through these openings is by no means impracticable.

I can scarcely suppose that quantum physicists are unaware of the errors of identification of observables which have been repeatedly pointed out in the last ten years; but they prefer to stick to the errors—presumably because they regard them as a lesser evil than a further encroachment of epistemology. As one of them has naïvely put it: "*Observable* is a very elusive conception, and if we pursue the criticism to the end, we shall have to doubt a lot of things we do not in the least want to doubt."

It appears then that, although the epistemological character of modern physical theories is recognised and at times strongly emphasised, there is not as yet a really effective union of scientific epistemology with science. I have been referring to the attitude of those who specialise on the fundamental problems. If we turn to the much larger circle of physicists who are occupied, not with developing, but with applying the results of the new theories, it is still more difficult to say where they stand. To what extent can the very general acceptance of the new theories be regarded as an acceptance of their epistemological outlook? It is still, I think, an unfamiliar idea among scientists that scientific philosophy should have any relation to scientific practice. If one writes of the heat-death of the universe, remarking that it is inescapable according to the second law of thermodynamics, some critic is sure to protest that this is an entire misconception of scientific law; a scientific law, he would say, is no more than an empirical generalisation valid over the range of space and time and circumstances for which it has been verified, and it is unscientific to extrapolate such a generalisation to an unknown distant future. Yet that same critic, if he were refereeing a paper on some new problem, such as a possible origin of cosmic rays in galaxies beyond the range of our telescopes, would assuredly look to see whether the proposed explanation was consistent with the second law of thermodynamics, and the paper would have small chance of acceptance if it was not.

When Einstein's theory arrived, which not only propounded a new epistemology but applied it to determine the law of gravitation and other practical consequences, physicists were puzzled how to classify it. Some argued that it was philosophy, *alias* metaphysics, and must be rejected out of hand. Others conceded that the formulae appeared to agree with observation and accomplished a valuable systematisation of knowledge, but believed that a "genuinely physical" interpretation of its meaning would in time supplant the epistemological jargon which at present envelops it. Fewer realised that the new epistemological outlook is the very heart of the theory, supplanting a fallacious system of thought which was barring progress. Even now we often find authors, who are by no means ignorant of the reasons for the change of thought, propounding theories for which they claim the advantage that they involve only Newtonian conceptions. As though it could be an advantage to incorporate a fallacious and obsolete view of the nature of observational knowledge!

This vagueness and inconsistency of the attitude of most physicists is largely due to a tendency to treat the mathematical development of a theory as the only part which deserves serious attention. But in physics everything depends on the insight with which the ideas are handled before they reach the mathematical stage.

The consequence of this tendency is that a theory is very commonly identified with its leading mathematical formulae. We continually find special relativity theory identified with the Lorentz transformation, general relativity with the transformation to generalised co-ordinates, quantum theory with the wave equation or the commutation relations. It cannot be too strongly urged that neither relativity theory nor quantum theory are summed up in fool-proof formulae for use on all occasions. A relativist is not a man who employs Lorentz-invariant formulae (which were introduced some years before the relativity theory appeared), but one who understands in what circumstances formulae ought to have Lorentz-invariance; nor is he a man who transforms equations into generalised co-ordinates (a practice at least a century old), but one who understands in what circumstances a special system of co-ordinates would be inapplicable. In quantum problems allowance must be made for the backward state of the theory; and the world is still awaiting a quantist who understands in what circumstances the standard wave equation and the commutation relations are applicable —as distinct from one who merely applies them and hopes for the best.

It is clear that no coherent philosophy can be made out of a half-and-half recognition of the place of epistemology in science. What really concerns our inquiry is that the leaders of physics have so far committed themselves in accepting its aid that its complete assimilation is only a question of time.

III

I do not see how anyone who accepts the theory of relativity can dispute that there has been some replacement of physical hypotheses by epistemological principles; nor do I think that those who accept the theory with understanding will be inclined to dispute it. The more controversial question is, How far can this replacement extend? Here my conclusion, based on purely scientific investigation, is much more drastic than that of most of my colleagues. I believe that the whole system of fundamental hypotheses can be replaced by epistemological principles. Or, to put it equivalently, all the laws of nature that are usually classed as fundamental can be foreseen wholly from epistemological considerations. They correspond to *a priori* knowledge, and are therefore *wholly subjective*.

I am sorry to have to put in the forefront what will generally be regarded as an individual scientific conclusion; but this cannot be avoided. I think I can see a clear philosophy emerging from the conclusion that the system of fundamental laws is wholly subjective. I cannot see any coherent philosophy emerging from the conclusion that some are subjective and some objective. Immediately I start on that line I am beset with objections and perplexities which I do not know how to meet. I do not condemn it on that account; perhaps with a great deal more thought a way of progress could be seen. But there is no inducement to spend my time trying to overcome the difficulties of a philosophy associated with scientific beliefs which I do not share. No one can contemplate entering on a difficult research based on premises which he has reason to believe erroneous. You will find plenty of philosophies of objective natural law; you will find here a philosophy of subjective natural law. If ever a philosophy of mixed subjective-objective natural law is developed, it will not be by me, for I am convinced that there is no scientific support for such a philosophy.

My conclusion, right or wrong, has a purely scientific basis. That it leads to a simple and rational philosophy is perhaps an argument in its favour; but that is an after-thought which did not weigh with me in reaching the scientific conclusion.

I did not set out with any preconceived idea of the scope of the epistemological method; and the conclusion that the whole of the fundamental laws of nature can be deduced from epistemological considerations was the result of trial.

Having had long associations with the theory of relativity, in which the method first showed its power, and seeing from time to time further opportunities for applying it, I found it was covering more and more of the ground of fundamental physics until at length the conclusion became irresistible.

One feature of this evidence needs to be emphasised. A law of nature is nowadays expressed by a mathematical equation. Our knowledge of the law can only be said to be complete if we know, not only the algebraic form of the equation, but the values of the parameters occurring in it. But it is customary to confine the term "law of nature" to the algebraic form, the parameters being referred to separately as "constants of nature". For example, the Newtonian theory of gravitation introduces a law, namely the inverse square law, and a constant, namely the gravitational constant; similarly for Einstein's theory. In the comparison of Newton's and Einstein's laws on p. 47, I have omitted all reference to the gravitational constant. But in the more far-reaching investigations to which I am now referring, the constants as well as the algebraic forms are included. My conclusion is that not only the laws of nature but the constants of nature can be deduced from epistemological considerations, so that we can have *a priori* knowledge of them.

Treating the scheme of natural law as a whole, as it is set out in the fundamental equations of physics, four constants of nature which are pure numbers★ are involved. These I find to be predictable *a priori*. I focus attention on these, because it is a more stringent test of the power of the epistemological method to provide a number (verifiable in some cases to about 1 part in 1000) than to provide forms of law. I think that the classical physicist had an inner feeling that the inverse square law was a natural form of

★ Formed by eliminating our three arbitrary units (centimetre, gram and second) from the seven constants of nature ordinarily recognised. (*New Pathways in Science*, p. 232.)

weakening of an effect by distance, which might be expected
a priori to apply to gravitation—though it would, of course,
be contrary to his principles to acknowledge any *a priori*
expectation. But he could scarcely have had an inner
intimation, acknowledged or unacknowledged, of the most
likely strength of such a force.

Now it is to be remembered that whatever is accounted
for epistemologically is *ipso facto* subjective; it is demolished
as part of the objective world. After a considerable number
of results have been found, there comes a time when we
pause to rest on our picks and judge, if we can, the extent
of the region marked out for demolition. Ordinary generalisation would have suggested much earlier that the region
was co-extensive with the fundamental laws (including
constants) of physics. But I could not bring myself to believe
the generalisation until the last of the four constants had
succumbed. I was held back by the common feeling, which
I now see was not philosophically well-grounded, that it was
necessary to leave at least one objective peg on which to
hang the subjective cloaks. Certainly an objective peg is
necessary, but we need not suppose that it has disguised itself
to resemble the cloaks.

One of the four natural constants is a very large number
called the *cosmical number*. It is perhaps most simply described
as "the number of particles in the universe", though it also
appears in physics in other more practical ways. We are
inclined to say that if anything is unforeseeable *a priori*, it is
the number of particles in the universe. This seems the inner-
most citadel of objectivity. But, after the work on the other
constants, the epistemological origin of this number was
comparatively easy to trace.

From a philosophical standpoint all the earlier work is
subsidiary to the attack on the cosmical number, which is the
real turning-point in our thought. So long as its objectivity
is outstanding, even if it is the only purely objective fact in

physics, we watch the exposure of subjective influences with equanimity. *Unification* we do not fear; and with one assuredly objective fact to point to, there is no danger of *nullification.* But when we find that the cosmical number is subjective—that the influence of the sensory equipment with which we observe, and the intellectual equipment with which we formulate the results of observation as knowledge, is so far-reaching that by itself it decides the number of particles into which the matter of the universe appears to be divided—not only do we lose the support on which we were relying, but there is no heart left in us to oppose the devouring flood of subjectivity any longer.

I shall accordingly deal at some length with the subjectivity of the cosmical number in Chapter XI. The actual derivation from epistemological considerations is, of course, much too technical to be given there. But in any case a mathematical demonstration carries no conviction if its result is "obviously impossible"; it only leads those who are sufficiently interested to look for a hole in the demonstration. I shall instead point out the way in which subjectivity has obtained a foothold in a region of thought from which one would have supposed it to be rigorously excluded; so that even the evaluation of the number of particles in the universe will be seen to be not obviously impossible.

I do not include atomic nuclei in this discussion of the laws of physics, because the present state of nuclear theory is comparable to the state of quantum theory before 1925, and provides no basis for philosophical inference. The filling of this gap does not seem very urgent. Hydrogen, it should be remembered, contains no nuclei (other than protons), so that it is fully covered by the present discussion.* Hitherto it has not occurred to anyone to advocate a philosophy idealist

---

* Including the non-Coulombian force which manifests itself in the close encounters of protons. Since this force also plays a large part in nuclear theory, the nucleus is to this extent included in the discussion.

as regards hydrogen and realist as regards oxygen; I think I may assume similarly that, in a study of the subjective or objective nature of the universe, its chemical composition is rather irrelevant.

I must mention here a point which ultimately turns out to be of great importance. The "law of chance" is not usually counted as a fundamental law of physics, and I do not include it among the laws that can be foreseen wholly from epistemological considerations. But according to the modern system of physics all our predictions of phenomena are predictions of what will probably happen, and are based on an assumption of non-correlation of the behaviour of individual particles which is derived from the law of chance. *Without an appeal to the law of chance physics is unable to make any prediction of the future.* The law of chance might therefore be claimed to be the most fundamental and indispensable of all physical laws. The reason why it is omitted is that, from the ordinary point of view, randomness is a negation of law; and it seems unnecessary to lay down a law saying that there is no law. But the ordinary view takes it for granted that the physical universe, and the particles into which we analyse it, are wholly objective; and the status of the law of chance (or non-correlation) requires reconsideration when applied to a partly subjective universe. It is impossible to treat this point fully until a late stage of the discussion. The view finally adopted will be found on pp. 180, 218. If in the meantime the reader finds my argument tending apparently to a more and more incredible conclusion, he may await a later twist that will soften it into something which will, I think, not too grossly affront his commonsense.

IV

Without further apology I shall now assume the reader's assent to the proposition that all the fundamental laws and constants of physics can be deduced unambiguously from *a priori* considerations, and are therefore wholly subjective. At least the onus of proof would seem to rest on those who claim objectivity for any law, thereby disturbing the homogeneity of the scheme without apparent necessity.

Let us go back to the analogy of the fish (p. 16) to illustrate the position now reached. When the ichthyologist rejected the onlooker's suggestion of an objective kingdom of fishes as too metaphysical, and explained that his purpose was to discover laws (i.e. generalisations) which were true for catchable fish, I expect the onlooker went away muttering: "I bet he does not get very far with his ichthyology of catchable fish. I wonder what his theory of the reproduction of catchable fish will be like. It is all very well to dismiss baby fishes as metaphysical speculation; but they seem to me to come into the problem."

I think that there is something in this objection. It perhaps underrates the power of the mathematician to handle selected material intelligently. But if our purpose is to determine laws of objective origin coming through to us in a form modified by subjective selection, I do not think the best way is to suppress all theories about the objective world—at any rate as working hypotheses. But at first sight the progress of physics seems to contradict this; for it was just when hypothesis about the objective world was abandoned, and we turned to a direct study of physical knowledge, that progress became astonishingly rapid.

The explanation is simple. All this progress relates to subjective law. It all relates to uniformities imposed on the results of observation by the procedure of observation. As for the type of uniformity illustrated by the ichthyologist's second generalisation that all sea-creatures possess gills—uniformities intrinsic in the world around us—we have not even made a beginning. The onlooker was right. No progress at all has been made with the kind of biological study that he had in mind.

I have alluded (p. 43) to a difficulty in defining the distinction between "fundamental" and "casual" hypotheses in physics. The same difficulty, expressed in a slightly different form, arises in making a rigid distinction between "laws of nature" and "special facts".

In classical physics this difficulty does not occur. Following Laplace, it is assumed that from the complete state of the universe at any one instant the complete state at any other instant, past or future, is calculable. The fundamental laws of nature are then defined to be the laws which, taken all together, furnish a sufficient set of rules for the calculation. To complete our knowledge of the universe we must know, besides the rules, the initial data to which they are to be applied. These data are the special facts.

It is possible that we may discover a rule or regularity applying to the special facts. If so, we should probably not deny it the title of a law of nature. But it can be distinguished from the fundamental laws of nature, because it is no part of the scheme of prediction. It is just a pattern of the special facts gratuitously incorporated in the design of the universe.

The distinction can be expressed very succinctly in mathematical language. The differential equations determining the progress of the universe are the fundamental laws of nature, and the boundary conditions are the special facts.

But this mode of distinction is possible only in a deterministic universe. In the current indeterministic system of physics, there is no corresponding demarcation between the laws and the special facts of nature. The present system of fundamental laws does not furnish a complete set of rules for the calculation of the future. It is not even part of such a set, for it is concerned only with the calculation of probabilities; and if ever the search for a scheme of definite prediction is renewed, it will be necessary to start again from the beginning on different lines. The part played by the special facts is also altered. The special facts, which distinguish the actual universe from all other possible universes obeying the same laws, are not given once for all at some past epoch, but are being born continually as the universe follows its unpredictable course. Moreover, in the differential equations of quantum theory the boundary conditions are not the objective facts but the knowledge we happen to possess about them.

The simple demarcation in classical theory between fundamental laws of nature and special facts is associated with determinism and cannot be carried over into the modern theory. But, approaching the question from the point of view of subjectivity, a new line of demarcation appears. We have found that the supposedly fundamental laws are wholly subjective. It is only reasonable that the part of our knowledge which is wholly subjective should be of a recognisably different type from that which involves the objective characteristics of the universe. It appears that this difference was not overlooked by the earlier physicists; and we find the region to be annexed to pure subjectivity already marked out under another name, viz. "fundamental".

The special facts, on the other hand, cannot be inferred from epistemological considerations and are not wholly subjective. It is the essence of our conception of a special fact that it might quite well have been otherwise—that there is no *a priori* reason why it should be what it is. It is true that many have held the view that the laws of nature might quite well have been otherwise; but they would scarcely assert that this is an inseparable part of the conception of a law of nature. Everyone recognises that it is in some sense taking a greater liberty with the universe to imagine the laws of nature to have been different than to imagine the special facts to have been different.

Results deducible by the *a priori* epistemological method are compulsory, and it is therefore impossible that the method should be extended to predict the special facts, which "might quite well have been otherwise". I am afraid that before I finish I shall have persuaded the docile reader to believe so many "impossible" things that the word will make little impression on him, and he will not jib at impossibility when I want him to. Let me then put the point rather differently. If by an advance of epistemological theory we succeed in predicting one of the so-called special facts in a wholly *a priori* way, we shall at once amend the classification: "Clearly we were mistaken in supposing that it was a special fact. Now that we see more clearly into its origin, we realise that there is a law of nature which compels it to be so."

The cosmical number affords a good example of such a change of view. Regarded as the number of particles in the universe, it has generally been looked upon as a special fact. A universe, it is held, could be made with any number of particles; and, so far as physics is concerned, we must just accept the number allotted to our universe as an accident or as a whim of the Creator. But the epistemological investigation changes our idea of its nature. A universe cannot be made with a different number of elementary particles— consistently with the scheme of definitions by which the "number of particles" is assigned to a system in wave-mechanics. We must therefore no longer look on it as a special fact about the universe, but as a parameter occurring in the laws of nature, and, as such, part of the laws of nature.

V

I must try to counteract the impression that the objective element in the physical universe, having, as it were, been driven into a corner before the advancing tide of subjectivity, now needs only perfunctory recognition. That impression is given in physics, because physics (in the narrow sense) is not interested in special facts except as data to be superseded by generalisations. Other physical sciences, such as astronomy, are not so exclusive, and to some extent restore the perspective. But the physical universe, as it affects us day by day, is not just a bundle of laws of nature; and the special facts are as important to us as the laws. Thus, although it is only through the special facts that we discern anything of the objective universe, it is a by no means empty view. Moreover, it is not as in the deterministic days when the special facts were collected into a single instant. Within the limits of the uncertainty principle they are ever-changing as the moments pass by.

The special facts are partly subjective and partly objective, depending partly on our procedure in obtaining observational knowledge and partly on what there is to observe. To separate the subjective or objective elements completely, we must consider laws; since a law or regularity may originate wholly in our procedure of observation or wholly in the objective world. It may be questioned whether we could ever isolate an objective law as completely as a subjective law, since it would have to be presented to us *via* our subjective forms of thought; but at least we could detect a regularity and recognise that its origin was objective, even if we could only describe it in subjective terms.

We are in danger of falling into a confusion regarding laws of nature—a confusion between what they are and what we originally intended them to be. To avoid ambiguity I will discriminate (temporarily) between "laws of nature" and "laws of Nature". Law of Nature will have the meaning that the term was originally intended to bear—a law emanating from the world-principle outside us, which we often personify as Nature. Law of nature will mean as heretofore a regularity which we have found in our observational knowledge, irrespective of its source. In short a law of nature is whatever would be designated by that name in current physical practice.

It will be seen that a law of Nature is a law of the objective universe. But all recognised laws of nature are subjective. We have thus reached the verbal paradox that no known law of nature is a law of Nature. Effectively the terms have become mutually exclusive.

It is true that we have left an opening. A law of Nature is a law of nature if it *would be* (not necessarily if it already *is*) accepted as such in physics. This brings me to a further question, Have we any reason to believe that if a law of Nature—a generalisation about the objective world—were to become known to us, it would be accepted by current physics as a law of nature? I think it would only be accepted if it conformed to the pattern of physical law that we are accustomed to. But this pattern is the pattern of subjective law. We shall try later to show by epistemological study how the pattern has grown out of the subjective aspect of physical knowledge. The pattern is the very hall-mark of subjectivity. Any expectation we may have formed that the objective laws of Nature, when they are discovered, will conform to the same pattern is quite unreasonable.

We must not attempt to lay down in advance the type of regularity which we call by anticipation a law of Nature. To assume that we know beforehand the pattern of objective law would be an assertion of *a priori* knowledge of the objective universe, repudiated by all schools of scientific thought. Not all our systematisation of knowledge is of the "exact" type employed in physical science; and in other sciences law has a broader interpretation. Hitherto it is only in the purely subjective part of our knowledge that we have found the *exact* type of law obeyed.

Perhaps it will be argued that although objective law, when it is discovered, may prove to be of an unfamiliar pattern, physicists will modify their ideas to accommodate it. The pattern of physical law has not remained immutable; and the pattern recognised to-day would not have been accepted in classical physics. If progress in the objective part of our knowledge makes it necessary to enlarge the pattern, it will not be the first time physics has undergone revolution. That is one possibility; but there is an alternative. Would the enlarged subject necessarily retain the name of physics? The former changes were compulsory; we did not drop classical physics solely because its field was too limited, but because we discovered its defects. But here the proposed change is not forced on us by a defect in the treatment of the subjective knowledge at present covered, but is for enlargement only. It might well be considered more appropriate to confine the name physics to the domain it at present occupies, and treat the new development as "outside physics". If so, the laws of Nature will never be the subject matter of physics.

This sounds like a quibble over names; but it gives a hint that may be really important. The suggestion is that when we succeed in making progress with the study of the objective world, the result will be very different from present-day physics, and that there is no particular reason to expect that it will be called physics. We have spoken of this as a development in the future; but may it not have occurred already? It seems to me that the "enlarged" physics which is to include the objective as well as the subjective is just *science*; and the objective, which has no reason to conform to the pattern of systematisation that distinguishes present-day physics, is to be found in the non-physical part of science. We should look for it in the part of biology (if any) which is not covered by biophysics; in the part of psychology which is not covered by psychophysics; and perhaps in the part of theology which is not covered by theophysics. The purely objective sources of the objective element in our observational knowledge have already been named; they are *life, consciousness, spirit*.

We reach then the position of idealist, as opposed to materialist, philosophy. The purely objective world is the spiritual world; and the material world is subjective in the sense of selective subjectivism.

CHAPTER V

EPISTEMOLOGY AND RELATIVITY THEORY

I

THE vocabulary of physics includes a number of terms such as length, energy, temperature, potential, refractive index, etc., which we call physical quantities. Relativity theory insists that all physical quantities shall be defined in a way which will enable us to recognise them in practical experience. A definition of potential must specify a way of determining potentials. A definition of length must specify a way of measuring lengths.

This demand is simply a recognition that if the theorist and the experimenter are to co-operate they must speak a common language. If we call in an experimenter to test the truth of our statements, his first question must be "How am I to recognise the thing you are talking about?" The answer we give him is its definition. If he verifies the truth of the statement, his certificate applies only so long as the words mean what we told *him* they did. To keep in reserve some other definition—some non-observational meaning— of the words in the statement, to be used after we have wangled the certificate, is dishonest. It is not less dishonest if we ourselves believe that the two definitions refer to the same thing; for the *belief* was not submitted to experimental test, and has not been certified.

Progress had been made towards this type of definition in pre-relativity days. At one time mass was defined as quantity of matter; but the experimenter was given no indication how he was to recognise the same "quantity of matter" when presented in different forms, e.g. wool and lead. Consequently, although it was not realised at the time, no state-ment about mass (unless restricted to one kind of matter) was ever verified experimentally. But later a definition of mass in terms of observable inertial properties was sub-stituted; and, with this changed meaning, observational test of the statements became possible. It has come to be the accepted practice in introducing new physical quantities that they shall be regarded as *defined* by the series of measuring operations and calculations of which they are the result. Those who associate with the result a mental picture of some entity disporting itself in a metaphysical realm of existence do so at their own risk; physics can accept no responsibility for this embellishment.

The innovation made by Einstein in his relativity theory was that the physical quantities involved in the measurement of space and time were brought under this rule. The reform was clearly necessary; for the experimenter is called upon to certify the truth of our conclusions about distances and intervals of time, just as much as he is called on to certify the truth of our conclusions about temperatures or magnetic fields. A definition of length which specifies a way of determining lengths observationally is indeed the most urgent requirement of all; for when we come to examine what is actually measured in any kind of experiment, it is nearly always a length or spatial measure—the length of a thread of mercury in a thermometer, the shift of a bright spot on a galvanometer scale, the displacement of a dark line in a spectrogram, etc.

It is strange that this innovation should have aroused an opposition, which is not even yet extinct. There still flourishes an unreasoning insistence that terms which have reference to measurement of space must not be connected with ob-servation in the same way that terms having reference to mechanical, optical, electromagnetic, thermal and other measurements are. There is a famous passage in the writings of Henri Poincaré, of pre-relativity date, which is often quoted in this connection:

If Lobatchewsky's geometry is true, the parallax of a very distant star will be finite. If Riemann's is true, it will be negative. These are results which seem within the reach of experiment, and it is hoped that astronomical observations may enable us to decide between the two geometries. But what we call a straight line in astronomy is simply the path of a ray of light. If, therefore, we were to discover negative parallaxes, or to prove that all parallaxes are higher than a certain limit, we should have a choice between two conclusions: we could give up Euclidean geometry, or modify the laws of optics, and suppose that light is not rigorously propagated in a straight line. It is needless to add that every one would look upon this solution as the more advantageous. Euclidean geometry, therefore, has nothing to fear from fresh experiments.*

Those who quote this passage have usually missed the moral. Clearly the moral is that the definition of the parallax or distance of a star must not be left to pure mathematicians whose assertions have nothing to fear from fresh experiments. It was true enough in Poincaré's time that theorists talked about distances which did not mean anything in particular, so that you were at liberty to choose whether they obeyed Euclidean or non-Euclidean geometry. But the experimenter went his own way and measured distances which meant something very particular—to the seventh or eighth significant figure. Theorist and experimenter did not speak the same language. Relativity theory instituted the obvious reform, and those happy-go-lucky days are over. Now, if a theorist reaches a conclusion about stellar or galactic distances, he does so with a proper fear of fresh experiments. I must admit having put forward conclusions of this kind, and I tremble every time a new experimental result is about to be announced. Not that I shall necessarily believe it.

* *Science and Hypothesis*, p. 72.

II

The definition of length or distance and the corresponding definition of time-extension are particularly important, because in general the definitions of other physical quantities presuppose that length and time-extension have been defined, and any ambiguity of their meaning would spread through the whole superstructure. If, instead of length being defined observationally, its definition were left to the pure mathematician, all the other physical quantities would be infected with the virus of pure mathematics.

Practical physicists have long been occupied with the accurate determination of lengths, and the principles which they strive to follow were settled before the theory of relativity arose. This branch of practical physics is called metrology. When therefore it became necessary to adopt formally an observational definition of length, there could be no question of setting up a rival procedure. The definition must give instructions as to a procedure of measurement of lengths. To the metrologist these instructions amounted simply to "Carry on".

It is not uncommon for writers to treat the definition of length or time-interval as though the meanings of these terms were freely at their disposal. But it is scarcely legitimate to adopt such an attitude towards terms in current use. A writer may perhaps claim to have fulfilled his obligations if he makes clear the meaning the term will have in his own writings, irrespective of the way it has been employed hitherto. But the common view is that it is reprehensible to use the term "white" to describe the appearance more usually known as "black"; and the practice, recently introduced by writers on kinematical cosmology, of giving to length and time a meaning which no Bureau of Standards would accept, though perhaps not amounting to moral obliquity, is a source of unnecessary confusion.

In all orthodox physical theory, the metrological practice
—or more strictly the principle which it attempts to carry
out—supplies the theoretical definition. Thus it is secured
that, when the experimenter checks the theorist, both are
referring to the same thing.

Accordingly, by length in relativity theory we mean what
the metrologist means, not what the pure geometer means.
In accepting relativity principles, the physicist puts aside his
paramour pure mathematics, dismisses their go-between
metaphysics, and enters into honourable marriage with
metrology. I am afraid those who represent the bride are
inclined to suspect that he is not entirely off with his first
love. Some writings on relativity look a bit mathematical.
Since I am not entirely convinced of the innocence of some
of my colleagues, I must on this point answer only for
myself. I declare that the suspicions are groundless. If I
sometimes employ pure mathematics, it is only as a drudge;
my devotion is fixed on the physical thought which lies
behind the mathematics. Mathematics is a useful vehicle for
expression and manipulation; but the heart of the theory is
elsewhere:

> Euphelia serves to grace my measure
> But Chloe is my real flame.

The crucial part of the definition of length is the specification of a standard which shall be available for comparison
at any place and at any time. Metrologists do not look upon
a particular bar of metal, such as the Paris metre, as an
ultimate standard; the mere fact that they feel anxiety as to
its permanence shows that they have in mind a more ideal
standard with which it might be compared. What is needed is
a physical structure, not necessarily permanent, but uniquely
reproducible. A calcite crystal whose length contains 10^8
lattice intervals will suggest the sort of standard required.

If that were specified as the standard of length, it could be reproduced in the farthest galaxy or at the remotest epoch of time.

Let us consider from a general point of view the problem of specifying a reproducible standard of length. Obviously we must not employ lengths in the specification; for that would be a vicious circle. Nor can we use any of the other "dimensional" physical quantities, for their definitions presuppose that standards of length, time and mass are already defined. The quantitative part of the specification must therefore consist of undimensional quantities, i.e. pure numbers. For example, the standard proposed above was specified by the number of lattice cells. We can, if we like, go farther and specify the chemical composition of the crystal by pure numbers, namely the atomic numbers of the elements concerned in it.

A purely numerical description of material structure is elaborated in quantum theory. The structure is described as consisting of a certain number of nuclei and electrons whose arrangement is specified by quantum numbers. Such a structure is necessarily unique from the observational point of view; for if two specimens showed observable differences, it would be taken as a proof that the existing theory of the structure was incomplete and additional quantum numbers would be introduced to distinguish them.

Thus the general answer to our problem is that any structure which is practically reproducible from a quantum specification will serve as standard. All such standards are equivalent, being in definite numerical ratios to the unit of length h/mc which appears in the fundamental equations of quantum theory.

The standard of time-extension is defined similarly. A spatial extension of the quantum-specified structure provides the standard of length; a time-periodicity of the same structure provides the standard of time-extension. The parallelism is closest if we employ a crystal; for, viewing the structure in four dimensions, periodicity is a lattice structure in time; and our two standards are respectively a specified number of space-lattice cells and a specified number of time-lattice cells of the crystal structure.

It is perhaps not superfluous to add that no question arises as to whether the standard of length defined in this way is *really* constant at all times and places. The question implies that we have in mind some more ultimate standard (invested with "reality") by which to define the delinquencies of the physical standard. The conception of physical quantities having to conform to some particular role allotted in advance in a vaguely imagined realm of reality, is not recognised in physical science; quantities such as length and time-extension are introduced solely for the purpose of succinct description of observational measurements actual or hypothetical.

III

We notice that relativity theory has to go outside its own borders to obtain the definition of length, without which it cannot begin. It is the microscopic structure of matter which introduces a definite scale of things. Since we have separated molar physics from microscopic physics primarily out of consideration of the grossness of our sensory equipment, it would be unreasonable to expect to find it complete in itself. We can only make it logically complete as far as the point where its roots stretch down into physics as a whole. Nor is microscopic theory, when separated from the rest, self-sufficient. The physical quantities pertaining to atoms, electrons, photons, which we talk about in microscopic theory, must also be given definitions which will enable the experimenter to measure them. But he does not measure them, and is not imagined even in hypothetical experiments to measure them, with atoms, electrons and photons; the statements of microscopic physics are not assertions of the results of such unimaginable experiments. The measurements are made with metre scales, micrometers, spectrographs—ultimately with our own gross sense-organs. Molar physics always has the last word in observation, for the observer himself is molar.

The secret of the union of molar and microscopic physics—of relativity theory and quantum theory—is "the full circle". They are not so much branches forking from one root as semi-circles joined at both ends. Generally we enter on the circle at the junction now under discussion, where relativity theory takes its standard of length from quantum theory. But relativity theory, which has made greater progress along its arc than quantum theory along its arc, is already exploring the other junction, where the cosmical constant and matters of that kind are involved. At this junction the roots of quantum theory penetrate into relativity theory, as at the other junction the roots of relativity theory penetrate into quantum theory. Only in combined relativity-quantum theory (not to be confused with current "relativistic quantum theory" which has unjustifiably usurped the name) can we exhibit the circle as a whole.

The failure to make relativity theory completely independent of quantum theory has one practical advantage. It has secured that the standard of length in relativity is the same as in quantum theory. The same ultimate standard is also recognised by the metrologists, who seek to realise it in the wave-length of cadmium light or the grating-space of calcite. Thus practical metrologists, relativity physicists and quantum physicists all mean the same thing when they speak of length or distance or time-interval. There is complete uniformity—except for a new-comer, the kinematical cosmologist, who considers that every one is out of step except himself.

It is often suggested that some of the constants of nature,

e.g. the velocity of light or the gravitational constant, vary with time. Unless the standards of length and time-extension have been carefully defined, such discussions are meaningless; and much that has been written on the subject is discounted by the fact that the writers are evidently unaware of the nature of the definition of these standards. Anyone who suggests variation of a fundamental constant has before him a heavy task of reconstruction of theory and reinterpretation of observational measurements before he can reach any observational confirmation or contradiction of his suggestion. Meanwhile I think that progress of the epistemological method has assured us that the constants of nature (apart from our arbitrary units) are numbers introduced by our subjective outlook, whose values can be calculated *a priori* and stand for all time. For this reason my personal conclusion is that there is no more danger that the velocity of light or the constant of gravitation will change with time than that the circumference-diameter ratio π will change with time.

Let us examine more closely what is implied in the suggestion that the velocity of light *in vacuo* changes with the time. An immediate consequence is that the ratio of the wave-length λ to the period T of any spectral line, say a hydrogen line, changes with time. Now for all epochs the standard of time is a time-period in some quantum-specified structure, and the standard of length is a space-extension in some quantum-specified structure. We may take this structure to be a hydrogen atom in the quantum-specified state in which it emits the line considered. It follows that either the ratio of the period of the emitted light to the time-period intrinsic in the emitting atom varies with time, or the ratio of the length of the emitted waves to the spatial scale of structure of the emitting atom varies with time. I do not think those who propose the variability of the velocity of light realise that, if their words have any meaning, they imply that the period of the light has no constant relation to—is therefore not determined by—any corresponding periodicity in its source; or alternatively, that the wavelength of the light has no constant connection with the linear scale of its source. If this were true, it would involve a conception of atomic structure so far removed from that of present-day quantum theory that scarcely anything in our present knowledge would survive.

IV

Thus far we have been considering how to define length unambiguously, but have not attended to the complications which may arise when extreme accuracy is required. We have been concerned to circumvent the clerkes in Chaucer's tale:

> Ye conne by argumentes make a place
> A myle brood of twenty foot of space.

These arguments still appear in scientific journals, particularly in reference to lengths and times at a remote cosmological epoch. It has, for example, been proposed to extend the rather uncomfortably cramped time-scale of the universe by making a logarithmic transformation of our time-reckoning:

> Lat see now if this place may suffyse
> Or make it roum with speche, as is youre gyse.

We now pass on to consider questions of extreme accuracy. Our quantum-specified standard is reproducible at the remotest times and places, and therefore satisfies the utmost demands of cosmological theory. Nevertheless, it has certain limitations. I will mention the two most important.

First, the quantum-specified standard does not provide an exact definition of length in strong electric or magnetic fields. This is because it is not strictly reproducible in such fields; a structure in an electromagnetic field cannot have precisely the same quantum specification as a structure in field-free conditions. We appeal in vain to the practical metrologist to arbitrate on this difficulty; he merely points out that, in using a standard of length, it is an elementary precaution to get rid of electric and magnetic fields. But it is idle to tell a man who is studying phenomena in a magnetic field that he must get rid of the field before making any measurements. Let us suppose that he wishes to measure the curvature of tracks of charged particles in a magnetic field. He will probably not be so ill-advised as to put the standard into the field; he will, for example, take a photograph of the tracks and measure the *photograph* with the standard. He must then use theoretical formulae to deduce the curvature of the tracks in the field from measurements of the photographs outside the field. But how is he to test whether his theoretical formulae are right? The indirect procedure is only justified if it is known to give the same results as a direct measurement would have done; but in this case, owing to the non-reproducibility of the standard, no direct procedure exists; and it cannot be claimed that the indirect procedure is known to give the same results as a *non-existent* direct procedure.

Since there are no precedent conventions to follow, a theorist concerned with exact equations in intense fields is free to introduce his own definition of length, provided only that it converges to the accepted definition as the field tends to zero. So much advantage has been taken of this freedom, that at least a dozen different "unified theories" of the gravitational and electromagnetic fields have been put forward each implying a slightly different definition of length. They are all of them right—right if the definition of length is adjusted to fit them. They will all of them be "confirmed by observation", because the inferences from measurements made outside the field, or the corrections to the measurements (if any) made inside the field, will be determined from the theory under test:

> There are nine and sixty ways of constructing tribal lays,
>   And every single one of them is right!

But, it may be said, will not quantum theory ultimately be able to calculate precisely how much a crystal standard expands or contracts when placed in a magnetic field, or how a wave-length is modified? We shall then merely have to apply the corrections for the change of the standard. I am afraid it is not quite so simple. Not even quantum theory can calculate a quantity which has not been defined. Undoubtedly quantum theory will find us a correction; but that only means that quantum theory, like the unified theories, has introduced (or will introduce) its own conventional definition. Doubtless a definition which commends itself to the quantum physicists will prevail in the end by *force majeure*; and indeed it is appropriate to leave the matter in their hands, since it was quantum theory that supplied our original definition. But it should be borne in mind that, although it is clearly necessary by some convention to extend the usual physical terminology to intense fields, whatever convention we adopt, the distances will be pseudo-distances (and similarly for all derived physical quantities, including the measure of the field itself), since they lack the most fundamental characteristic of the metrological conception of length, namely the correspondence between similarity of length and similarity of physical structure.

V

The second limitation is that the standard must be *short*. A long standard will not work except in very special circumstances.

Suppose we try to measure the diameter of the earth with

a long crystal standard stuck through it like a knitting needle through an orange. It is well known that the earth is strained out of shape by the tide-raising forces of the sun and moon; the long crystal will likewise be strained. A practical metrologist would insist on removing the sun and moon (and earth) before delicate measurements were attempted, since it is an elementary precaution that the standard must not be subjected to strain. We may express the objection more formally by pointing out that the strain means that the structure of the crystal no longer has the specification prescribed in the definition of the standard.

We cannot always remove the bodies that are causing the strain. If we are measuring up the solar system, we cannot begin the proceedings by clearing away the sun. Thus, in general, we have to be content with short standards which are proportionately less affected by strain. With the short standard we can only measure short distances directly. To a first approximation we can determine large distances by measuring them in short sections, and summing or integrating the results;* but to a higher approximation this method also leads to ambiguous results. This ambiguity is known as the *non-integrability of displacement.*

It is worth noticing that there is a direct observational test which would show that the long crystal rod no longer had the prescribed structure. If, for example, a singly refracting crystal were chosen, the strain would be indicated by the appearance of double refraction. The point of this remark is that the non-reproducibility of a long standard, and our consequent inability to define non-infinitesimal distances accurately, is a fact which might have been discovered by direct observation, instead of being deduced from our knowledge of tide-raising forces in gravitational theory. This is

* That is to say, we *define* a large distance as the result of integrating short distances (provided that the result is unambiguous) instead of defining it as the result of a comparison with a long standard.˙

important, because presently we shall use the indeterminacy of long distances as a foundation for gravitational theory, instead of deducing it as a consequence of the theory.

For the survey of a large region we have to develop a system of metrical description in which only the infinitesimal distances are observational data. This is a technical problem of differential geometry, which we need not discuss here. For simplicity I have omitted reference to time; but similar considerations apply to the four-dimensional space-time world.

The failure to define long distances observationally, or in mathematical language the non-integrability of displacement, is the foundation of Einstein's theory of gravitation. According to the usual outlook gravitation is the cause of the trouble; gravitation produces the strains which render long standards useless. But Einstein's outlook is more nearly that the "trouble"—the non-integrability of displacement—is the cause of gravitation. I mean that in Einstein's theory the ordinary manifestations of gravitation are deduced as mathematical consequences of the non-integrability of displacement. I cannot enter here into the details, which require a large treatise; but the gist of it is that Einstein showed how to specify the non-integrability quantitatively, and used the numbers thus introduced—the famous $g_{\mu\nu}$—as a measure of the influence which disturbs the ideal conditions in which displacements would be integrable. "Gravitational field" is the name which we have given to this influence. As might be expected, this systematic specification of the gravitational field has been found to be more precise than the casual specification of it by one of its effects which happened to strike Newton's attention when he sat under an apple-tree.

Einstein's specification is more accurate than Newton's; but that the two refer to the same thing is seen when we recall that it was the strain, produced by the two ends of the long standard trying to fall with different accelerations towards the sun or moon, which vitiated it as a standard and frustrated our effort to measure directly an integrated length. We need therefore not be surprised that from Einstein's specification the more ordinary manifestations of gravitation in falling bodies can be deduced.

This is a particularly good example of the way in which epistemological study has brought about a great advance in science; and it is worth while to recall the principal steps. If physics is to describe what we really observe, we must overhaul the definitions of the terms employed in it so that they explicitly refer to observational facts and not to metaphysical conjectures. Length and time interval in particular need to be carefully defined, since they are the basis of nearly all other physical definitions. To avoid circular definitions it is essential that the standards of length and time interval should be the extensions of structures completely specified by pure numbers. With such structures as standard we obtain a definition of infinitesimal intervals (in the absence of an electromagnetic field), but we do not obtain an exact definition of long intervals. Thus, in order that physics may express purely observational knowledge, it is necessary to develop a system of description of the location of events based wholly on infinitesimal distances and time intervals; we thereby avoid reference to long intervals which have no exact observational definition. This system of location, depending on infinitesimal intervals, is the foundation of general relativity theory. In relativity theory a long distance is in general an approximate conception only; it is incapable of exact definition.*

As soon as we realise that the definition of length does not cover long distances and so does not imply integrability

* The breakdown of the ordinary definition leaves the term at the disposal of investigators, and various technical definitions of long distances have been proposed. But these technical uses of the term are irrelevant here.

of displacement, integrability becomes a special hypothesis which requires defending. One does not accept hypotheses gratuitously. Proceeding from this rational basis of space-time measurement we find that the phenomenon of gravitation appears automatically—unless we deliberately introduce a hypothesis of integrability to exclude it—and in this way we are led immediately to Einstein's theory of gravitation.

VI

I have been continually emphasizing the subjectivity of the universe described in physical science. But, you may ask, was it not the boast of the theory of relativity that it penetrated beyond the relative (subjective) aspect of phenomena and dealt with the absolute? For example, it showed that the usual separation of space and time is subjective, being dependent on the observer's motion, and it substituted a four-dimensional space-time independent of the observer. It may seem difficult to reconcile this view of Einstein's theory as lifting the veil of relativity which hides the absolute from us, with my present account of modern physics as acquiescing in, and making the best of, a partially subjective universe.

It is necessary to remember that there has been thirty years' progress. Relativity began like a new broom, sweeping away all the subjectivity it found. But, as we have advanced, other influences of subjectivity have been detected which are not so easily eliminated. Probability, in particular, is frankly subjective, being relative to the knowledge which we happen to possess. Instead of being swept away, it has been exalted by wave mechanics into the main theme of physical law.

The subjectivity referred to in these lectures is that which arises from the sensory and intellectual equipment of the observer. Without varying this equipment, he can vary in position, velocity and acceleration. Such variations will produce subjective changes in the appearance of the universe to him; in particular the changes depending on his velocity and acceleration are more subtle than was realised in classical theory. Relativity theory allows us to remove (if we wish) the subjective effects of these *personal* characteristics of the observer; but it does not remove the subjective effects of *generic* characteristics common to all "good" observers— although it has helped to bring them to light.

Confining attention to the personal, as distinguished from the generic, subjectivity, let us see precisely what is meant by removing this subjectivity. There does not seem to be much difficulty in conceiving the universe as a three-dimensional structure viewed from no particular position; and I suppose we can, after a fashion, conceive it without any standard of rest or of non-acceleration. It is perhaps rather unfortunate that it is, or seems to be, so easy to conceive; because the conception is liable to be mischievous from the observational point of view. Since physical knowledge must in all cases be an assertion of the results of observation (actual or hypothetical), we cannot avoid setting up a dummy observer; and the observations which he is supposed to make are subjectively affected by his position, velocity and acceleration. The nearest we can get to a non-subjective, but nevertheless observational, view is to have before us the reports of all possible dummy observers, and pass in our minds so rapidly from one to another that we identify ourselves, as it were, with all the dummy observers at once. To achieve this we seem to need a revolving brain.

Nature not having endowed us with revolving brains, we appeal to the mathematician to help us. He has invented a transformation process which enables us to pass very quickly from one dummy observer's account to another's. The knowledge is expressed in terms of tensors which have a fixed system of interlocking assigned to them; so that when one tensor is altered all the other tensors are altered, each in a determinate way. By assigning each physical quantity to an appropriate class of tensor, we can arrange that, when one quantity is changed to correspond to the change from dummy observer A to dummy observer B, all the other quantities change automatically and correctly. We have only to let one item of knowledge run through its changes—to turn one handle—to get in succession the complete observational knowledge of all the dummy observers.

The mathematician goes one step farther; he eliminates the turning of the handle. He conceives a tensor symbol as containing in itself all its possible changes; so that when he looks at a tensor equation, he sees all its terms changing in synchronised rotation. This is nothing out of the way for a mathematician; his symbols commonly stand for unknown quantities, and functions of unknown quantities; they are everything at once until he chooses to specify the unknown quantity. And so he writes down the expressions which are symbolically the knowledge of all the dummy observers at once—until he chooses to specify a particular dummy observer.

But, after all, this device is only a translation into symbolism of what we have called a revolving brain. A tensor may be said to symbolise absolute knowledge; but that is because it stands for the subjective knowledge of all possible subjects at once.

This applies to personal subjectivity. To remove the generic subjectivity, due say to our intellectual equipment, we should have similarly to symbolise the knowledge as it would be apprehended by all possible types of intellect at once. But this could scarcely be accomplished by a mathematical transformation theory. And what would be the result if it were accomplished? According to Chapter IV, if we remove all subjectivity we remove all the fundamental laws of nature and all the constants of nature. But, after all, these subjective laws and facts happen to be important to beings who are not equipped with revolving brains and variable intellects. And if the physicist does not take charge of them, no one else is qualified to do so.

Even in relativity theory, which deals with the absolute (in a somewhat limited sense), we continually hark back to the relative to examine how our results will appear in the experience of an individual observer. We are not so eager now as we were twenty years ago to eliminate the observer from our world view. Sometimes it may be desirable to banish him and his subjective distortion of things for a time, but we are bound to bring him back in the end; for he stands for—ourselves.

CHAPTER VI

EPISTEMOLOGY AND QUANTUM THEORY

I

I MUST still keep hammering at the question, What do we really observe? Relativity theory has returned one answer—we only observe *relations*. Quantum theory returns another answer—we only observe *probabilities*.

Considered epistemologically, probability is a very peculiar conception; for a precise and certain knowledge of a probability is construed as a rough and uncertain knowledge of something of which it is the probability. This seems to conflict with our comfortable assurance that knowledge is knowledge, and facts are facts. Probability is commonly regarded as the antithesis of fact; we say "This is only a probability, and must not be taken as a fact". But, if the answer of quantum theory is right, the "hard facts of observation" are probabilities. What we mean is that the result of an observation, though undoubtedly a fact in itself, is only valuable scientifically because it informs us of the probability of some other fact. These secondary facts, known to us only through probability, form the material to which the generalisations of physics refer.

We may assume that current theory is right in its conclusion that our measurements determine only the probabilities of the quantities and entities which figured in classical physics; so that the probability conception necessarily intrudes in a comparison of the newer with the classical ideas. But it is perhaps not obvious that a probability interpretation is essential when we are seeking to develop the new outlook on its own independent basis. The results of observational measurement *can* be construed as a hazy and uncertain knowledge of the entities of classical physics; but does not that mean that we should abandon the classical entities, and introduce more fundamental entities of which observation gives us precise and certain knowledge? The suggestion is that in the new physics the so-called probabilities are actually the real entities—the elemental stuff of the physical universe. We have precise knowledge of *them*; and it would seem retrogressive to postulate other entities behind them of which our knowledge must always be uncertain.

I think that this idea is at the back of a rather common suggestion that a proper reformulation of our elementary concepts would banish the present indeterminism from the system of physics. The idea is that the indeterminism revealed by the new physics is not intrinsic in the universe, but appears only in our attempt to connect it with the obsolete universe of classical physics. Probability would then be merely the funnel through which the new wine is poured into old bottles.

But the suggestion overlooks the essential feature of the indeterminism of the present system of physics, namely that the quantities which it can predict only with uncertainty are quantities which, *when the time comes*, we shall be able to observe with high precision. The fault is therefore not in our having chosen concepts inappropriate to observational knowledge. For example, Heisenberg's principle tells us that the position and velocity of an electron at any moment can only be known with a mutually related uncertainty; and, taking the most favourable combination, the position of the electron one second later is uncertain to about 4 centimetres. This is the uncertainty of the prediction from the best possible knowledge we can have at the time. But one second later the position can be observed with an uncertainty of no more than a fraction of a millimetre. It has often been argued that the impossibility of knowing simultaneously the exact position and exact velocity only shows that position and velocity are unsuitable conceptions to use in expressing our knowledge. I have no special attachment to these conceptions; and I will grant, if you like, that our knowledge of the universe at the present moment can be regarded as perfectly determinate (the supposed indeterminacy being introduced in translating it into an inappropriate frame of conception). But that does not remove the "indeterminism" (which is distinct from the "indeterminacy"), namely that this knowledge, however expressed, is inadequate to predict quantities which, independently of our frame of conception, can be directly observed when the time comes.

Returning to the more general aspect of the probability conception, we find that it cannot be got rid of by any transformation of outlook. It is not possible to transform the current system of physics, which by its equations links probabilities in the future with probabilities in the present, into a system which links ordinary physical quantities in the future with ordinary physical quantities in the present, without altering its observable content. The bar to such a transformation is that probability is not an "ordinary physical quantity". At first sight it appears to be one; we obtain knowledge of it from observation, or from a mixture of observation and deduction, as we obtain knowledge of other physical quantities. But it is differentiated from them by a peculiar irreversibility of its relation to observation. The result of an observation determines definitely a probability distribution of some quantity, or a modification of a previously existing probability distribution; but the connection is not reversible, and a probability distribution does not determine definitely the result of an observation. For an ordinary physical quantity there is no difference between making a new determination and verifying a predicted value; but for probability the procedures are distinct.

Thus we may expand the answer of quantum theory that "we only observe probabilities" into the form: The synthesis of knowledge which constitutes theoretical physics is connected with observation by an *irreversible* relation of the formal type familiar to us in the concept of probability.

We shall later (p. 96) have to consider the epistemological reasons which have made it necessary for theoretical physics to proceed in this way, rather than by adhering to the formulation of a universe whose contents have a reversible relation to observation. But for the present we shall simply accept the modern theory as the result of *a posteriori* examination of observational knowledge, and try to understand the nature of the irreversibility displayed in it.

II

The following example will help to make clear the irreversibility associated with probability. We have two similar bags A and B; A contains two white balls and one red, B contains two red balls and one white. We draw a ball from one of the bags, and find that it is white. It can be deduced that the chances are 2 to 1 that the bag is A. Similarly the drawing of a red ball indicates that the chances are 2 to 1 that the bag is B. Now suppose that we are handed one of the bags with the information that the chances are 2 to 1 that it is the bag A; what will be the result of drawing a ball? Reversibility would require the answer to be definitely a white ball; for if a red ball is drawn it shows that the chances are 2 to 1 that the bag is B—contrary to the information stated. But this answer is, of course, quite wrong; the correct answer is that the chances are 5 to 4 in favour of white.

Let us call the probability that the bag is A the *A-ness* of the bag. A certain observational procedure applied to the bag (drawing a ball) can be used to measure the A-ness. Of the two possible results x and y of the procedure, x indicates an A-ness $\frac{2}{3}$, and y an A-ness $\frac{1}{3}$. But if the procedure is applied to a bag whose A-ness is known to be $\frac{2}{3}$, the result is not necessarily x. This is in contrast to an ordinary physical

quantity. If we were determining the weight instead of the
A-ness, and from the results or readings x and y we could
infer weights 1 gm. and 2 gm., respectively, it is axiomatic
that a weight already known to be 1 gm. would give the
reading x, not y.

Another contrast may be noticed. Suppose that from the
result of an observation we have determined the value x of a
physical quantity. If we repeat the observation and obtain
the same result, we take it as confirming the value x.
But it is not so with probability. By drawing a ball we
determined the A-ness of the bag to be $\frac{2}{3}$. If we repeat the
drawing and obtain the same result (namely white), instead
of taking this as a confirmation, we alter the value $\frac{2}{3}$ to $\frac{4}{5}$!
The A-ness indicated by drawing two white balls in suc-
cession is $\frac{4}{5}$.

To show that the same irreversibility applies to probability
as it is actually used in modern physical theories, we may
contrast the probability waves treated in quantum theory
with sound waves. According to wave mechanics, an
observation determines or produces a concentrated wave
packet in the probability distribution. This wave packet
diffuses according to laws embodied in the equations of the
theory; and we can calculate the form into which the wave
packet will have spread one unit of time later. *But the theory
does not assert that this is the form of wave packet which would be
produced by an observation made one unit of time later.* On the
other hand, if from the observationally determined form of a
sound wave at one instant we calculate the form into which
it will have spread one unit of time later, the whole point of
the theory is that we obtain the form which would be determined by observations made one unit of time later.★

★ The parallelism is obscured by the fact that we speak of the form of
the sound wave as "observationally determined", and the form of the
probability wave as "observationally produced". This difference of
phrasing is itself a recognition of the distinction between a reversible and
an irreversible relation to observation.

Apart therefore from any other implications of probability, we may distinguish it formally as a name given to something which has a relation to observational knowledge different from that of ordinary physical quantities—an irreversible instead of a reversible relation. This absolute difference will remain however we change the nomenclature; and it will be seen that the hope of getting back to something like the classical system of physics by renaming the probabilities as entities cannot be fulfilled.

The entire system of laws of physics at present recognised is concerned with probability, which, we have seen, signifies something that has an irreversible relation to observation. As a means of calculating future probabilities the laws form a completely deterministic system; but as a means of calculating future observational knowledge the system of law is indeterministic. The irreversibility ensures that, though we put definite observational knowledge into the deterministic machine, we cannot take definite observational knowledge out of it. Hence, as regards observational content, the system of modern physics is indeterministic.

We have said (p. 10) that every item of physical knowledge must be an assertion of what would be the result of carrying out a specified observational procedure. It is now necessary to add that it is a qualified assertion claiming only a certain degree of probability. Strictly speaking, the Court of Appeal should be asked to decide, not whether the assertion is true, but whether it has the degree of probability claimed for it. Usually, however, we submit to observational test assertions which claim to have so high a probability as to be "practically certain". Low probabilities can only be given a statistical test. This means that the individual assertion of low probability is replaced by a statistical consequence which has very high probability—high enough to be rated as practically certain—and the latter is tested by observation.

Thus the Court of Appeal is only called upon to judge assertions claimed as practically certain.

Remembering that every item of physical knowledge must assert the result of an observational procedure, we have to inquire what is the observational procedure whose result is asserted when we have physical knowledge that the probability of a stated event is $\frac{1}{3}$. The only observational procedure in any way associated with this knowledge is the statistical test above-mentioned, which consists of determining the frequency in a large class of events of a similar kind to the particular event stated. We have already condemned the immorality of claiming observational knowledge of one thing when we have actually tested something different. The statistical assertion must therefore be regarded, not as deduced from the assertion of low probability, but as explaining what a low probability actually means; that is to say, the assertion of low probability must be understood to assert the result of the statistical test, although verbally it appears to refer to a single event. Whatever significance probability may have in other departments of thought, in physical science probability is essentially a statistical conception; that is to say, it is *defined* as a frequency in a class of events.

The term "probability" is often used, without statistical implications, in reference to the strength of our expectation or belief. When used in this sense it cannot form part of a scientific assertion, since the assertion would be rendered thereby incapable of observational test. But it can still be used to qualify the assertion as a whole—to describe our confidence or lack of confidence that the assertion would be confirmed if submitted to observational test. It is important to distinguish this non-quantitative use of the term from its technical scientific use as an observationally determinable quantity.*

---

* For other aspects of the problem of probability in physics, see *New Pathways in Science*, Chapter VI.

III

Probability, which was first introduced into theoretical physics in connection with thermodynamics and the kinetic theory of gases, has been of increasing importance in later developments, and is now firmly embedded as one of the most fundamental concepts. We have seen that, owing to its irreversible relation to observation, it is distinguishable from other physical quantities. We cannot eliminate this irreversibility by any change of our conceptual frame of thought. If we should decide that it ought to be rooted out of physics, the only way is to abandon the present system of physics and build up a new one from the beginning. This brings us to a consideration of the *a priori* aspect of the problem. If we consider the way in which observational knowledge is obtained and formulated, at what point does it become a matter of necessity or of expediency to deviate into probability? The answer is not so elementary as we might at first expect. It seems as though it ought not to be difficult to formulate observational knowledge as a precise description of a universe without using the probability conception; and it is by no means easy to put one's finger on the flaw in such an attempt.

It is first necessary to recall the implicit understanding that by "observation" is meant *good* observation. To define a physical quantity we must specify a procedure which will give a good measurement of it. But we have now to introduce a new point. "Good" is not here to be taken to mean "perfect". By *good* observation we emphatically do not mean *perfect* observation.

The trouble is not that in practice all our measurements are more or less imperfect. It would certainly be untrue to say that the basis of current physical knowledge is perfect observation. But this is only a formal criticism, which we may consider to have been adequately countered by the ordinary theory of errors of observation. If the probability concept in physics had been confined to the theory of errors of observation, it would not have been of any great concern to us here. But it has penetrated much more deeply into the roots of physics.

The serious difficulty appears when we consider what the definition of a perfect observation implies. We require, not only perfect appliances and perfect skill, but perfect conditions—free from disturbing influences. To complete the definition the perfect conditions must be specified in terms of observation. It is not sufficient to say that all disturbing influences must be eliminated; we cannot decide whether an outside influence is a disturbance or part of the standard conditions for a perfect observation, unless the standard conditions of perfect observation have been defined.

A good experimenter rearranges things in the neighbourhood of the system he is studying. He surrounds it with a thermostat; he shields it from radio-active substances; he counteracts the earth's magnetic field. These are his efforts to secure standard *good* conditions. A good observer is—a bit fussy. A perfect observer would be intolerable. For his standard *perfect* conditions he would want to rearrange the stars and improve the universe out of recognition.

The odd thing is that, having made his perfect arrangements, the perfect observer often fails to accomplish things which to the good observer are quite elementary. Here is a simple test. He is asked to put a gram of hydrogen at 0° C. into a spherical vessel of 5 cm. radius, and measure the pressure. The good experimenter will do this without difficulty; but the perfect experimenter, having tried several times and obtained widely different answers each time, gives it up and announces that the pressure is quite indeterminate. The reason is that in making the interior surface of the vessel not merely a good sphere but a perfect sphere, he has removed those useful little roughnesses which dissipate any angular momentum the gas may possess when it is put in. Consequently the gas in each experiment was left with an arbitrary rotation, and the measured pressures differed accordingly. In striving after perfection the observer only achieved indeterminacy.

Various *contretemps* of this kind await the perfect observer who is working alone; but if another perfect observer joins him, the result is chaos. Each of them, in order to secure the perfect conditions for his own experiment, will insist on removing the apparatus set up by the other. The observer of lengths smooths out the universe, so that no asymmetrical influence may distort his standards; whereupon the observer of angular directions complains that his landmarks have been removed, and the universe made so symmetrical that there is no recognisable point to measure from.

One perfect observer is a nuisance. Two perfect observers make a fight. Three perfect observers send us fleeing for refuge to the concept of probability.

Whilst one perfect observer is engaged in the primary observation giving the main quantity or reading, an army of perfect observers must be testing the conditions under which the observation is being made so that the proper corrections may be applied if they are found to be imperfect. Possibly they might be able to do this without interfering with the primary observer; but, being perfect observers, they too will require perfect conditions for their measurements, and these conditions must be checked by a further batch of perfect observers. The result is a perfect anarchy—observers fighting to remove each other's apparatus, interfering with each other's experiments, trying to make every particle in the universe respond to half a dozen tests at once. To avoid this fiasco of perfection, we must be content to compromise, and trust a little to luck as well as measurement. And so we get a system of physics in which luck (probability) and measurement are associated together.

It is well known that the interference of different kinds of measurement is the source of Heisenberg's uncertainty principle, which is the epistemological gateway by which the probability conception enters quantum theory.

IV

The almost universal practice of using the term "an observation" for what would be more properly described as "an item of observational knowledge" is liable to cause confusion in philosophical discussions. Consider, for example, an observation of the apparent magnitude of a star. If we are asked to state the precise nature of this observation, we give an account of the photometric procedure by which the result, say $11^{m}.42$, is reached. But this result is not in itself an item of observational knowledge, or at least not an item of scientific value. We knew beforehand that among the myriads of stars some would almost certainly have the magnitude $11^{m}.42$. The valuable item of observational knowledge is that a star *whose identity has been recorded* has the magnitude $11^{m}.42$. The observational procedure by which this knowledge is derived includes the observations necessary to identify the star as well as those which measure stellar brightness.

In *The Nature of the Physical World* I introduced the term "pointer reading" to describe the general nature of exact observation.* Whatever quantity we say we are "observing", the actual procedure nearly always ends in reading the position of some kind of indicator on a graduated scale or its equivalent. The pointer reading is an observation in the strict sense; but it does not by itself constitute an item of observational knowledge, which is probably the more usual meaning of the word. In a rather well-known example in *The Nature of the Physical World*, in referring to our observational knowledge that "the mass of the elephant is two

* P. 251; "Everyman" edition, p. 244.

tons", I identified "two tons" with the reading of the pointer when the elephant was placed on a weighing machine; but the knowledge that the mass two tons is the mass of the elephant is not acquired by paying attention solely to the movement of the pointer.

More generally we must recognise that an item of observational knowledge involves, besides a primary pointer reading, secondary pointer readings identifying the circumstances in which the primary pointer reading occurred. It must be admitted that even an isolated pointer reading is an item of knowledge of a sort; but it is not with such items that the scientific method deals. For scientific knowledge the association with other pointer readings is an essential condition; and we may therefore describe physical knowledge as a knowledge of the associations of pointer readings.

The secondary pointer readings are "co-ordinates" (in a generalised sense) of the primary pointer reading. When, for example, we determine the intensity of a magnetic field, we associate with it the time and the co-ordinates in space of the point to which the determination applies. The magnetic intensity is then the primary pointer reading, and the co-ordinates in space and time are the secondary pointer readings. But the chain of pointer readings does not stop here. Tertiary pointer readings are required to identify the system of co-ordinates used, and to determine its metric; but these tertiary readings are common to all items of knowledge referred to the co-ordinate frame, and (unlike the secondary pointer readings) are not determined afresh for every primary reading. There is considerable economy in using a systematic plan of identification such as a space-time co-ordinate system; for otherwise a long regression of pointer readings may be necessary to connect the primary pointer reading with other elements in our physical knowledge.

In *The Nature of the Physical World* it is emphasised that physical knowledge is concerned with the connection of pointer readings rather than with the pointer readings themselves; and it is concluded that the connectivity of pointer readings, as expressed by the laws of physics, supplies the common background which realistic problems always demand—the background described by the tertiary pointer readings which are not determined afresh for each individual item of knowledge. But, if I may venture to criticise the author of that book, he does not seem to have appreciated the difficulty which arises through the interference of pointer readings with one another when we contemplate such an unlimited multiplicity of pointer readings. It is true that the interference is negligible in molar physics (to which the discussion in *The Nature of the Physical World* was limited). But in a fundamental discussion of this kind it is not legitimate to separate molar physics from microscopic physics; for we have seen (p. 76) that neither branch is logically complete in itself.

Our definition of the physical universe is that it is the world which physical knowledge is formulated to describe. The interference of observations creates a difficulty which must be met in one of two ways. Either we must take the complete description of the physical universe to embody more than the totality of our possible knowledge of it; so that, whichever of two interfering observations we choose to make, there will be a place for it in the description. Or we must adopt a *flexible* universe containing nothing which is not represented by our actual knowledge (or in theoretical discussions by the supposedly actual knowledge furnished as data of the problem considered). In the first alternative we cannot consistently suppose all the items of the complete description to be represented by actual pointer readings; and it is therefore not true to say that its structure is a connectivity of pointer readings. The second alternative is adopted in wave mechanics, which accepts as leading features of the physical universe the probability waves created by actual observation of the physical quantities with which they are associated. Clearly there is no more than a formal distinction between the study of a universe flexible according to the knowledge we happen to have of it and a direct study of the knowledge itself. Either alternative brings us back to the conclusion that the common background is required to connect one item of knowledge with the rest of knowledge, rather than one element of an external universe with the rest of the universe.

V

We have reached a point at which it is desirable to take stock of our position. The following summary will recall the principal conclusions that we have so far reached:

(1) Physical knowledge (by definition) includes only knowledge capable of observational test; an item of physical knowledge must therefore assert the result of a specified observational procedure.

(2) The definitions of the terms used in expressing physical knowledge must be such as to secure that (1) is satisfied. In particular the definition of a physical quantity must specify unambiguously a method of measuring it.

(3) Strict adherence to (2) involves a number of modifications of the conceptions and practice of classical physics; and indeed there still survive glaring violations of it in current quantum theory. The points (4) to (9) below arise when the definitions are scrutinised from this point of view.

(4) The first definitions required are those of length and time-interval, since the definitions of other physical quantities presuppose these. The standards of length and time must be structures specified by pure numbers only (since no other quantitative terms are available at this early stage). This means that the standards must be reproducible from a quantum specification.

(5) Only short standards, suitable for measuring infinitesimal displacements in space and time, are provided by such specifications; and it must not be assumed that the infinitesimal displacements so measured are integrable.

(6) Owing to the interference of exact observations with one another, an attempt to define observationally the exact conditions under which the measurement of a physical quantity is intended to be carried out breaks down. It is therefore necessary to leave the minor details to chance.

(7) In this way the probability conception is incorporated in the fundamental definitions. It introduces an irreversible relation between observation and formulated observational knowledge. This irreversibility makes the existing system of physics indeterministic, considered as a system of prediction of what can be observed at a future time.

(8) Certain quantities used in the formulation of physical knowledge in classical physics are found to have no definition satisfying (2). These are unobservables, e.g. absolute simultaneity at a distance.

(9) Other quantities, conditionally observable, have been employed in conditions in which they are unobservable. For example, the definition of relative co-ordinates presupposes that the particles are distinguishable, but ordinary relative co-ordinates are still used erroneously in problems concerning indistinguishable particles.

(10) The conclusions (4) to (9) are reached by considering the way in which physical knowledge is obtained and formulated. We refer to them as epistemological or *a priori* conclusions, to distinguish them from *a posteriori* conclusions derived from a study of the results of observations which have been obtained and formulated in this way.

(11) Although epistemological conclusions are of the nature of truisms, they have far-reaching consequences in physics. Thus the unobservability of absolute simultaneity (8) leads to the special theory of relativity; the non-integra-

bility of displacement (5) leads to Einstein's theory of gravitation; the introduction of the probability conception in a fundamental way (7) leads to the method of wave mechanics.

(12) In the modified theories which result, epistemological principles play a part which was formerly taken by physical hypotheses, i.e. generalisations suggested by an *a posteriori* study of the results of observation.

(13) Current relativity theory and quantum theory, as usually accepted, have not yet taken full advantage of this epistemological method. It appears that when the epistemological scrutiny of definitions is systematically applied, and its consequences are followed up mathematically, we are able to determine all the "fundamental" laws of nature (including the purely numerical constants of nature) without any physical hypothesis.

(14) This means that the fundamental laws and constants of physics are wholly subjective, being the mark of the observer's sensory and intellectual equipment on the knowledge obtained through such equipment; for we could not have this kind of *a priori* knowledge of laws governing an objective universe.

(15) It is not suggested that the physical universe is wholly subjective. Physical knowledge comprises, besides "laws of nature", a vast amount of special information about the particular objects surrounding us. This information is doubtless partly objective as well as partly subjective.

(16) The subjective laws are a consequence of the conceptual frame of thought into which our observational knowledge is forced by our method of formulating it, and can be discovered *a priori* by scrutinising the frame of thought as well as *a posteriori* by examining the actual knowledge which has been forced into it.

(17) The characteristic form of the fundamental laws of physics is the stamp of subjectivity. If there are also laws of

objective origin, they may be expected to be of a different type. It seems probable that wherever effects of objective governance have appeared they have been regarded as an indication that the subject is "outside physics", e.g. conscious volition, or possibly life.

(18) Epistemological laws (if correctly deduced) are compulsory, universal, and exact. Since the fundamental laws of physics are epistemological, they have this character—contrary to the view usually advocated in scientific philosophy, which has assumed that they are merely empirical regularities.

The next four chapters will be devoted to a more intensive study of the conceptual frame of thought referred to in (16). This will show more directly the way in which the subjective element enters into physical science, and help to justify the name "Selective Subjectivism" which we have given to the scientific system of philosophy.

CHAPTER VII

DISCOVERY OR MANUFACTURE?

I

ABOUT 270 years ago a historical experiment was performed in this college (Trinity College) which was considered to demonstrate the composite nature of white light. The account of the discovery, in the leading text-book of my undergraduate days, is:*

> It was still supposed that every refraction of light actually produced colour, instead of merely separating the colours already existing in ordinary white light, but in 1666 Newton made the important discovery of the actual existence of colours of all kinds in solar light, which he showed to be no other than a compound of the various colours, mixed in certain proportions with each other and capable of being separated by refraction of any kind.

It seems a simple matter to demonstrate that the white light of the sun is really a mixture of light of various colours. But suppose that, instead of proving it to a docile student, we have to prove it to a spiritualist who watches everything we do with the same suspicion that we should feel it our duty to adopt in investigating his claims. We begin by taking a spectroscope—a prism spectroscope would be more closely reminiscent of Newton, but we happen to have got hold of a grating spectroscope and it is not worth while to change it. We let a ray of sunlight fall on one end of the instrument, and invite the spiritualist to apply his eye to the other. He is astonished to see a brilliant green light which, we tell him, the spectroscope has separated out from the other colours present in white sunlight. Suspecting trickery, he examines each part of the instrument. He pounces on a gadget scratched

* Preston, *Theory of Light*, 2nd ed., p. 9.

with thousands of fine parallel lines. Triumphantly he realises how it works. The light falls obliquely so that the parallel lines reflect it, not simultaneously, but one after the other. A single incident pulse is thus multiplied by reflection into thousands of pulses following at regular intervals. Evidently this has been arranged to produce the particular periodicity which our eyes recognise as green colour. The claim that the green colour (i.e. green periodicity) already existed in the sunlight was false; we had hidden in the instrument a device, which we hoped he would not discover, for introducing the green periodicity. The spiritualist goes away confident that he has exposed a clumsy fraud.

By using a grating, instead of a prism which acts more mysteriously, we gave the show away. As mentioned in the above quotation, it was the prevailing view before Newton that the prism actually produces the colour; so that the essential part of Newton's demonstration was a series of experiments believed to prove that the prism does not produce the colour but separates it. These we were going to show the spiritualist; but it is no good showing them now. These further experiments work as well with a grating as with a prism; and whatever they prove for the prism they prove for the grating. It is useless to appeal to them as supporting a conclusion which, in the case of the grating, we see to be untrue.

I think it not unlikely that even an expert might fall into this trap to-day—such is the glamour of a historic experiment. He really knows better; but one does not always recall one's knowledge when it is wanted. The position was made plain by Rayleigh and Schuster, and is indeed part of the usual optical teaching. White light, such as sunlight, is a quite irregular disturbance with no tendency to periodicity. But mathematically we can analyse any disturbance, however irregular, into the sum of periodic Fourier components; and we can, if we like, think of the disturbance as made up of these components. Whether the spectroscope *sorts out* a particular periodicity or *impresses* it, is just a matter of expression. The idea of "sorting" is appropriate, because the spectroscope would fail to impress the particular periodicity on light in which the corresponding Fourier component happened to be missing; and in fact the solar spectrum shows dark lines where the white light fails to take the impress of the corresponding periodicity, owing to certain Fourier components having been sifted out of the light before it reaches us. But the idea of "impressing" the periodicity is also appropriate; for we should not expect an impress to take on unsuitable material, and the Fourier analysis may be regarded as the mathematician's preliminary test to see if the material will bear the impress. It is particularly appropriate when a grating is used, since "impressing the periodicity" is then a plain elementary statement of the *modus operandi*.

The mistake was not in saying that a green component already exists in the sunlight, for that is at any rate a legitimate way of thinking, but in claiming that we could decide experimentally between two equally permissible forms of description. And, by our oversight, it happened that the form of description we condemned was rather more natural and appropriate than the one we undertook to defend.

The realisation that natural white light is a quite irregular disturbance, into which regularity is introduced by our method of spectroscopic examination of it, was the first sign of an uneasiness among physicists as to whether in our experiments we may not interfere so much as to destroy what we were seeking to investigate. The uneasiness has become more acute in modern atomic physics, since we have no tool fine enough to probe an atom without grossly disturbing it.

The question I am going to raise is—how much do we discover and how much do we manufacture by our experiments? When the late Lord Rutherford showed us the atomic nucleus, did he *find* it or did he *make* it? It will not affect our admiration of his achievement either way—only we should rather like to know which he did. The question is one that scarcely admits of a definite answer. It turns on a matter of expression, like the question whether the spectroscope finds or whether it makes the green colour which it shows us. But since most people are probably under the impression that Rutherford found the atomic nucleus, I will make myself advocate for the view that he made it.

II

The tendency of writers on quantum theory has been perhaps to go farther than I do in emphasising the *physical* interference of our experiments with the objects which we study. It is said that the experiment puts the atoms or the radiation into the state whose characteristics we measure. I shall call this Procrustean treatment. Procrustes, you will remember, stretched or chopped down his guests to fit the bed he had constructed. But perhaps you have nor heard the rest of the story. He measured them up before they left next morning, and wrote a learned paper "On the Uniformity of Stature of Travellers" for the Anthropological Society of Attica.

The physical violence, however, is not really the essential point. Ideally the experimenter might wait until the conditions of his experiment happened naturally, as those engaged in the observational sciences are forced to do. We grossly interfere with the irregularity of white sunlight by passing it through a spectroscope; but sunlight may occasionally fall through a crevice on to a natural crystal and form a spectrum without our help. The standard conditions, which turn aimless measurement into a good measurement of a definite physical quantity useful for scientific induction, may sometimes occur without human interference. But, so far as physical theory is concerned, it makes no difference whether we *create* or whether we *select* the conditions which we study. Whether the interference of the observer is physical or selective, it is none the less marked in the resulting conclusions. The kind of observation on which physical theory is based is not a casual taking notice of things around us, nor a general running round with a measuring rod. Under cover of the term "good" observation the bed of Procrustes is artfully concealed.

To what length can this interference be carried? I do not think that any limit can be set *a priori*. It is pertinent to remember that the concept of substance has disappeared from fundamental physics; what we ultimately come down to is *form*. Waves! Waves!! Waves!!! Or for a change—if we turn to relativity theory—curvature! Energy which, since it is conserved, might be looked upon as the modern successor of substance, is in relativity theory a curvature of space-time, and in quantum theory a periodicity of waves. I do not suggest that either the curvature or the waves are to be taken in a literal objective sense; but the two great theories, in their efforts to reduce what is known about energy to a comprehensible picture, both find what they require in a conception of "form".

Substance (if it had been possible to retain it as a physical conception) might have offered some resistance to the observer's interference; but form plays into his hands. Suppose an artist puts forward the fantastic theory that the form of a human head exists in a rough-shaped block of marble. All our rational instinct is roused against such an anthropomorphic speculation. It is inconceivable that Nature should have placed such a form inside the block. But the artist proceeds to verify his theory experimentally—with quite rudimentary apparatus too. Merely using a chisel to separate the form for our inspection, he triumphantly proves his theory. Was it in this way that Rutherford rendered concrete the nucleus which his scientific imagination had created?

Do not be misled by thinking of the nucleus as a sort of billiard ball. Think of it rather as a system of waves. It is true that the term "nucleus" is not strictly applicable to the waves (cf. the electron, p. 51): but it is equally unrigorous to speak of the nucleus as having been "discovered". The discovery does not go beyond the waves which represent the knowledge we have of the nucleus.

Does the sculptor's procedure differ in any essential way from that of the physicist? The latter has a conception of a harmonic wave form which he sees in the most unlikely places—in irregular white light, for example. With a grating instead of a chisel, he separates it from the rest of the white light and presents it for our inspection. Just as the sculptor separates the rough block of marble into a bust and a heap of chips, so the physicist separates the irregular wave disturbance into a simple harmonic green wave and a scrap-heap of other components. In Fourier and other recognised methods of analysis, physics allows and practises the splitting of form into components. It allows us to select a form which *we ourselves* have prescribed, and treat the rest as contamination which we can remove, if we can devise the necessary apparatus, so as to exhibit our selected form by itself. In every physical laboratory we see ingeniously devised tools for executing the work of sculpture, according to the designs of the theoretical physicist. Sometimes the tool slips and carves off an odd-shaped form which we had not expected. Then we have a new experimental discovery.

It is difficult to see where, if at all, a line can be drawn. The question does not merely concern light waves, since in modern physics form, particularly wave form, is at the root of everything. If no line can be drawn, we have the alarming thought that the physical analyst is an artist in disguise, weaving his imagination into everything—and unfortunately not wholly devoid of the technical skill to realise his imagination in concrete form.

An illustration may show that a serious practical question is raised. Just now nuclear physicists are writing a great deal about hypothetical particles called *neutrinos* supposed to account for certain peculiar facts observed in β-ray disintegration. We can perhaps best describe the neutrinos as little bits of spin-energy that have got detached. I am not much impressed by the neutrino theory. In an ordinary way I might say that I do not believe in neutrinos.* But I have to reflect that a physicist may be an artist, and you never know where you are with artists. My old-fashioned kind of disbelief in neutrinos is scarcely enough. Dare I say that experimental physicists will not have sufficient ingenuity to *make* neutrinos? Whatever I may think, I am not going to be lured into a wager against the skill of experimenters under the impression that it is a wager against the truth of a theory. If they succeed in making neutrinos, perhaps even in developing industrial applications of them, I suppose I shall have to believe—though I may feel that they have not been playing quite fair.

The question is raised whether the experimenter really provides such an effective control on the imagination of the theorist as is usually supposed. Certainly he is an incorruptible watch-dog who will not allow anything to pass which is not observationally true. But there are two ways of doing that—as Procrustes realised. One is to expose the falsity of an assertion. The other is to alter things a bit so as to make the assertion true. And it is admitted that our experiments *do* alter things.

* Doubtless until a truer understanding of the spin problem is reached, it is better to make shift with neutrinos than to ignore the difficulty which they are intended to meet. I have no objection to neutrinos as a temporary expedient, but I would not expect them to survive—except that, as suggested in this paragraph, survival may not be wholly a .question of intrinsic merit.

I have been acting as advocate for an extreme view, presuming that your natural prejudices are all the other way. I must now try to recover the poise of a judge. I do not think that *as yet* the analytical imagination of the mathematical physicist has developed into the unfettered imagination of the artist. He plays the game according to certain rules which, arbitrary as they may seem at first sight, express an epistemological principle that goes deep into the roots of human thought. This we shall discuss presently. But have we a guarantee that the rules are for all time? The boy who outrageously breaks the rules of a game may be suitably punished by his companions, or he may be commemorated as the founder of Rugby football. The man who makes neutrinos will not be punished if he has overstepped the rules; he will be acclaimed for freeing physics from an obstruction to its useful development.

However, our concern is with the characteristics of present-day physics and not with what it may become in future. We shall now enter on a very extensive subject of discussion, namely the nature and origin of the rules which distinguish the methods of the physicist from the free imagination of the artist.

CHAPTER VIII

THE CONCEPT OF ANALYSIS

I

In introducing subjective selection (p. 16), I attributed it to "the sensory and intellectual equipment" used in obtaining observational knowledge. The inclusion of *intellectual* equipment may have seemed surprising. It is easy to see that our sensory equipment has a selective effect—that the nature and extent of our knowledge of an external world must be largely conditioned by its lines of communication with consciousness, provided by our sense organs. It is not so obvious that within the mind there is any further selection at work on the material thrust upon it by the sense organs.

It must, I think, be agreed that all that comes into consciousness as the result of stimulation of the sense organs is knowledge of a kind. It is not possible to perceive without knowing that we perceive; and perception implies "knowledge of our perceptions as such". But we are here concerned with *physical knowledge*, which is an abbreviation for knowledge acquired by the methods of physical science (p. 2). Introspective examination of our perceptions *as such* is no part of the method of physical science. An intellectual activity begins when we relate our perceptions to one another. The result of this activity is a synthesis of perception, and a formulation of knowledge of a different type from knowledge of individual perceptions as such. Knowledge of the relatedness of sensory perceptions, e.g. the sound of thunder following the flash of lightning, is the beginning of science. The rudiments of the method of physical science are, of course, employed long before any systematic study of what is going on around us is attempted; and even the most unsophisticated apprehension of phenomena involves commonsense as well as sense—that is to say, an intellectual as well as a purely sensory activity of consciousness.

We have already paid attention to this intellectual speciali-sation of physical knowledge, in pointing out that the acquirement of observational knowledge means something more than observation in the elementary sense of taking notice. We have seen that, for refined scientific develop-ments, what is required is good (though not perfect) obser-vation of defined quantities. There is a big gap between this and the passive reception of sensory impressions; and in this gap the selective influences of our intellectual equipment have their opportunity. If we consider the sequence, ob-jective event—perception—physical knowledge, there is a double sifting, firstly by our sensory equipment, secondly by our intellectual equipment. In the present epistemological treatment we start from knowledge, so that the order is reversed, and it is the intellectual sifting that first comes under consideration.

In analysing this intellectual activity, I shall make use of the phrase "form of thought"; or, when the form is in some degree elaborated, "frame of thought". This may be regarded as a predetermined form or frame into which the knowledge we acquire observationally is fitted. For example, a very deep-rooted form of thought is that which formulates the knowledge acquired by observation as a description of a world. Every item of physical knowledge is fitted into this form of thought, and deemed to be a descriptive fact about a universe. So prevalent is this form that knowledge which is not concerned with the relatedness of sensory perceptions is often forced into it, and treated as a descriptive fact about a non-material world—a spiritual world. I do not think the reasons for or against employing this form of thought are stronger in the one case than in the other. Whatever we have to apprehend must be apprehended in a way for which our intellectual equipment has made provision.

The epistemological method of investigation leads us to study the nature of the frame of thought, and so be forewarned of its impress on the knowledge that will be forced into it. We may foresee *a priori* certain characteristics which any knowledge contained in the frame will have, simply because it is contained in the frame. These characteristics will be discovered *a posteriori* by physicists who employ that frame of thought, when they come to examine the knowledge they have forced into it. Procrustes again!

These foreseeable characteristics are not by any means trivial; they are laws or numerical constants which physicists have been at great pains to determine by observation and experiment. As an example we may take the law of increase of mass with velocity, which has been the subject of many famous experiments. It is now realised that this law automatically results from the engrained form of thought which separates the four-fold order of events into a three-fold order of space and an order of time. When knowledge is formulated in a frame which compels us to separate a time dimension from the four-fold order to which it belongs, a component called the mass is correspondingly separated from the four-fold vector to which it belongs; and it requires no very profound study of the conditions of separation to see how the separated component is related to the rest of the vector which prescribes the velocity. It is this relation which is rediscovered when we determine experimentally the change of mass with velocity.

In one sense the outlook of relativity theory has emancipated us from the frame of thought which separates a time dimension from the rest of the four-fold order; and the law of variation of mass with velocity should have disappeared from physics, since it refers to conceptions associated with a discarded frame. The fact which corresponds to it in the new frame of thought is an obvious truism which does not require separate mention. But a glance at the literature of modern physics shows that the law has not disappeared; and its importance is just the same as when the highest skill of the experimenter was being applied to determine it empirically. The real position is that by the outlook of relativity we "see through" the form of thought, but we do not actually discard it—except temporarily in specialised researches where its distorted view would be a hindrance. The law of change of mass with velocity therefore retains its place as a scientific conclusion; and it is by no means a trivial conclusion. The test of triviality must be whether the result appeared trivial before we understood its real nature. Even the production of a rabbit from a hat is a trivial phenomenon if you know how it is done.

It is not possible to specify a particular frame of thought as the frame prevailing consistently throughout present-day physics. We must in any case distinguish between the frame of thought which corresponds to the outposts of modern theory and the frame which furnishes most of our current vocabulary. The latter is more or less the same as that which corresponds to familiar apprehension of things around us. But even familiar apprehension does not adhere consistently to any one frame of thought. For example, looking down from the top of a sky-scraper, we see a number of tiny objects walking about in the street below. The inference that they are objects of normal human stature, made to appear small by distance, is not a matter of immediate apprehension; it is a considered interpretation of what we apprehend. But for objects near to us, the scientific frame has become the familiar frame. When a man walks away from us in a room, we do not "see" him getting smaller. We see, or think we see, an object of constant size changing its distance from us; and it is only by an effort of introspection that we convince ourselves that the visual image is becoming smaller.

Since it is part of the art of physics to employ the common forms of thought as servants when they cease to be our masters, it is scarcely accurate to speak of them as having been discarded. It is better to say that the advance of physics has emancipated us from some of the common forms of thought. We use them, but we are not deceived by them.

II

The modern theories of physics have emancipated us from certain traditional forms of thought. That is why they seem so revolutionary. Is this the end of the advance, or do there remain in our outlook other forms of thought obstructing progress from which future physicists will succeed in freeing themselves? And if so, can the emancipation be continued indefinitely, or is it approaching a limit in which the surviving forms will be the bare necessities of thought?

We shall examine some of the forms of thought which still remain unchallenged in the scientific outlook. We are suspicious of the phrase "necessities of thought"; for scientific thought has grown accustomed to doing without many of its alleged necessities. But, whether necessities or not, the forms we are about to discuss have a hold on us which seems incomparably stronger than any we have hitherto thrown off.

For a scientific outlook I think the most fundamental of all forms of thought is the *concept of analysis*. This means the conception of a whole as divisible into parts, such that the co-existence of the parts constitutes the existence of the whole. In a formal definition I should not use the term "existence", since it refers to a concept which is probably less elementary than the concept of analysis. But a formal definition is not required in referring to a form of your own thoughts. My description is sufficient for you to recognise the form I mean, and that is all that is needed.

The point which I must emphasise is that I am referring to the conception of *a set of parts*, not to the individual conception of *a part*. In the concept of analysis a part is always a member of a complete set of parts, and its significance is bound up with the system of analysis in which it occurs. We could, if necessary, express this relation of a part to a system of analysis by using the term "component"; but that perhaps savours too much of mathematical terminology for the present very general application.

At first sight my insistence that a part must always be associated with analysis into a complete set of parts seems an idle formality. We can recognise that the head is part of the body without referring to a systematic anatomical classification of the parts of the body. To fulfil the formal requirement of the concept of analysis, we can say that the head is a part of the body associated with a system of analysis which divides the body into two parts, namely the head and the rest of the body. But since that applies to any arbitrarily selected part of anything, the reference to a system of analysis becomes a tautology.

To explain why we have to start from the notion of a complete set of parts rather than from the apparently simpler notion of a single part, I must ask a question. Is the bunghole of a barrel part of the barrel? Think well before you answer; because the whole structure of theoretical physics is trembling in the balance.

Suppose that the answer is Yes. Then the actual barrel is to be regarded as consisting of an unperforated barrel together with a hole—a closed wooden structure together with a minus quantity of wood. It is not a question whether this expresses an absolute truth. The question is whether it is a form of thought which we shall permit ourselves to employ. In this form of thought one of the parts, namely the unperforated barrel, is more than the whole. Euclid in his innocence thought that "the whole is greater than the part"; but Euclid was not acquainted with modern physics.

Our answer has made the term "part" meaningless in itself. Whatever A and B may stand for, A is always part of B; since our form of thought admits the division of B into two parts, namely A and $B - A$. The term "part" can therefore only be usefully employed for the parts which are associated with a system of analysis, and the whole significance of a part is associated with the system of analysis in which it appears. It conveys nothing to say that A is a part of B; but it conveys something to say that A is one of the parts appearing in a specified system of analysis applied to B.

Next suppose that we adhere to Euclid's axiom and decide that the bung-hole of a barrel is not part of the barrel. The objection to this is that it has long ceased to be the form of thought employed in physics. It is, I think, really a compound association of two concepts, the concept of analysis and the concept of substance. The concept of substance introduces a clear distinction of positive and negative; so that we can have a limited form of the concept of analysis, which we may call substance-analysis, in which the systems of analysis are restricted to those which furnish a complete set of *positive* parts. When the analysis is not associated with substance (or with a structurally equivalent concept), when for example it is associated with wave form, the restriction cannot be imposed. In optics darkness is considered to be constituted of two interfering light waves; light may be a "part" of darkness. In Fourier analysis the components partially cancel one another in the manner of positive and negative quantities. Thus, although there may be cases in physics in which analysis is applied to entities which by definition are essentially positive and the restriction of substance-analysis applies, we now look on it as an incidental restriction in a particular application and not as part of the fundamental concept of analysis.

That the general form of the concept of analysis is the form accepted in physical science is shown conclusively by the example of the positron. A positron is a hole from which an electron has been removed; it is a bung-hole which would be evened up with its surroundings if an electron were inserted. But it would be out of the question nowadays to define "part" in such a way that electrons are parts of a physical system but positrons are not.

You will see that the physicist allows himself even greater liberty than the sculptor (p. 111). The sculptor removes material to obtain the form he desires. The physicist goes further and adds material if necessary—an operation which he describes as removing negative material. He fills up a bung-hole, saying that he is removing a positron. But he still claims that he is only revealing—sorting out—something that was already there.

Once again I would remind you that objective truth is not the point at issue. We must not make the mistake, illustrated at the beginning of Chapter vii, of trying to decide by crucial experimental test between what are only two different forms of expression. I dare say you have a battery of arguments to prove to me by irrefutable logic that the bung-hole is not part of the barrel. But this is quite irrelevant; it will only show that you do not use (except by inadvertence) the term "part" with quite as much generality of meaning as the physicist does.

Our purpose is to expose, not necessarily to justify, the frame of thought underlying the expression of our physical knowledge. Partially at least we emancipate ourselves from a frame of thought as soon as we realise that it is only a frame of thought and not an objective truth we are accepting. Any power for mischief it may have is sterilised so long as it is kept exposed. I would not like to say that the concept of analysis is a necessity of thought, though it appears to be a necessity of any form of scientific thought. But, whether it is a necessary form or not, it has dominated the development of present-day physics, and we have to follow up its influence on the scheme of description of phenomena which has resulted.

III

It is clear that the concept of analysis as applied in physics must have been specialised according to some guiding principle; otherwise there would not be the same general agreement as to the products of analysis of the physical world, namely molecules, atoms, protons, electrons, photons, etc. There is another engrained form of thought which has selected the system of analysis to be applied in physics. I will call this specialisation of the concept of analysis the *atomic concept*, or for greater precision the *concept of identical structural units*.

The new conception is, not merely that the whole is analysable into a complete set of parts, but that it is analysable into parts which resemble one another. It is at the opposite pole from the analysis, say, of a human being into soul and body, in which the two parts belong to altogether different categories of entities. I will go farther, and say that the aim of the analysis employed in physics is to resolve the universe into structural units which are *precisely* like one another.

It may be objected that the structural units recognised in present-day physics, though resembling one another to a certain extent, are not precisely alike. The Fourier components of white light, though all simple harmonic trains of waves, differ in wave-length—a difference which we observe as difference of colour. But this difference is not intrinsic. It depends on the relation of the observer to the structural unit; if he recedes from the source of light, green light turns to red. Intrinsically the constituents of light—the wave trains or the photons—are all precisely alike; it is only in their relations to the observer, or to external objects generally, that they differ. That is the essence of the relativity theory. All the variety in the world, all that is observable, comes from the variety of relations between entities. Therefore, when we reach the consideration of the intrinsic nature or structure of the entities that are related, there is nothing left but sameness—in so far as that nature or structure comes within the scope of physical knowledge and is part of the universe which physical knowledge describes.

Granting that the elementary units found in our analysis of the universe are precisely alike intrinsically, the question remains whether this is because we have to do with an objective universe built of such units, or whether it is because our form of thought is such as to recognise only systems of analysis which shall yield parts precisely like one another. Our previous discussion has committed us to the latter as the true explanation. We have claimed to be able to determine by *a priori* reasoning the properties of the elementary particles recognised in physics—properties confirmed by observation. This would be impossible if they were objective units. Accordingly we account for this *a priori* knowledge as purely subjective, revealing only the impress of the equipment through which we obtain knowledge of the universe and deducible from a study of the equipment. We now say more explicitly that it is the impress of our frame of thought on the knowledge forced into the frame.

We have just seen that the concept of identical structural units is implicit in the relativity outlook, which attributes variety to relations and not to intrinsic differences in the relata; but I suppose it would be too much to claim that the relativity outlook is engrained in us—that our minds are so constituted that we cannot help moulding our thoughts in the Einsteinian way. I want to show therefore that the concept of identical structural units expresses a very elementary and instinctive habit of thought, which has unconsciously directed the course of scientific development. Briefly, it is the habit of thought which regards variety always as a challenge to further analysis; so that the *ultimate* end-product of analysis can only be sameness. We keep on modifying our system of analysis until it is such as to yield the sameness which we insist on, rejecting earlier attempts (earlier physical theories) as insufficiently profound. The sameness of the ultimate entities of the physical universe is a foreseeable consequence of forcing our knowledge into this form of thought. That it is really engrained in us can be seen from the following example.

Analysis of matter, as usually presented in present-day theory, reaches a considerable degree of homogeneity of the ultimate parts, but does not quite attain the ideal. We find protons exactly like one another; we also find electrons, like one another but differing from protons. Thus the physicist recognises two varieties of elementary units; and nowadays it is difficult to restrain him from adding several others. Why does a proton differ from an electron? The answer suggested by relativity theory is that they are actually similar units of structure, and the difference arises in their relations to the general distribution of matter which forms the universe. The one is related right-handedly and the other left-handedly. This accounts for the difference of charge; and the difference of mass is also (in a more complicated way) a difference of relation to the external matter without which there would be no means of determining mass observationally. There is no reasonable doubt that this answer is correct; but what interests us here is not the scientific answer resulting from the application of relativity theory, but the way in which we instinctively try to account for the difference. We cannot allow ourselves to think of the difference between a proton and an electron as an irreducible dualism—like the difference between soul and body. (I use the best comparison I can find; but the form of thought, which insists on getting behind—on explaining—variety, is so universal that even the dualism of soul and body is challenged by it.) No sooner do we discover a difference between protons and electrons than we begin to wonder what makes them different. When this question arises, we always fall back on structure. We try to explain the difference as a difference of structure, the structure of the proton being presumably the more complicated. But if protons and electrons possess structure, they cannot be the ultimate units of which structure is built. Therefore the present variety of the end-products of physical analysis is an indication that we have not yet touched bottom; and we must push our investigations farther, till we reach identical units which will not challenge us to farther analysis. The inference, as it happens, is fallacious, because the difference between protons and electrons is in the external relations and is not intrinsic. But a fallacious inference is informative as to our background of thought; and the thought which insists on intruding is that things which differ do so because they have different structure. The difference resides in the structure and not in the units out of which structure is built.

I conclude therefore that our engrained form of thought is such that we shall not rest satisfied until we are able to represent all physical phenomena as an interplay of a vast number of structural units intrinsically alike. All the diversity of phenomena will then be seen to correspond to different forms of relatedness of these units or, as we should usually say, different configurations. There is nothing in the external world which dictates this analysis into similar units, just as there is nothing in the irregular vibrations of white light which dictates our analysis of it into monochromatic wave trains. The dictation comes from our own way of thought which will not accept as final any other form of solution of the problem presented by sensory experience.

In current quantum theory the analysis approaches, but has not yet reached, this ideal. For that reason quantum physicists are still unsatisfied that they have got to the bottom of the relationships of the various kinds of particle that they recognise, and of the connection between gravitation, electromagnetism and quantisation. For my own part I think that the account given in most books on quantum theory by no means represents the full extent of our present knowledge of this problem. If more attention is paid to the relativity side of the problem, the main outline of the extension of physical theory from the present halting-point of quantum theory to the ultimate structural units is fairly clear. A general account of the development of a rational system of physics, starting from the structural units, is given on pp. 162–169. For fuller details of the steps by which from this beginning we are able to deduce the accepted laws and constants of nature, reference must be made to my mathematical treatise.★

IV

It is usually implied in the concept of analysis that the parts are self-sufficient. A part can, without violence to thought, be conceived as existing without the other parts which abut it. Or, to put it more rigorously, we can conceive a whole which, when subjected to the system of analysis we are employing, would yield no more than this one part. The theoretical physicist employs this conception of self-sufficiency when, in order to investigate the structure of an atom, he removes from consideration the whole universe except this one atom.

But here there arises a conflict of conception. If a part, e.g. an atom, were just what it would be without the rest of the universe, and the rest of the universe were just what it would be without this one atom, our bodies (which form part of the rest of the universe) are just what they would be without this atom, and we can therefore have no sensory experience in any way connected with or emanating from the atom.

★ *Relativity Theory of Protons and Electrons* (Cambridge, 1936).

The conception of permanently self-sufficient parts of the physical universe is self-contradictory; for such parts are necessarily outside observational knowledge, and therefore not part of the universe which observational knowledge is formulated to describe.

The model structure of an atom is incomplete unless it contains some provision by which *we* can become aware of what is happening in the atom. In short, physics having taken the world to pieces, has the job of cementing it together again. The cement is called *interaction*.

One of the most remarkable achievements of current quantum theory is the way it has surmounted the difficulty of giving to the parts of the universe a kind of self-sufficiency which does not cut them off from interaction with the rest of the universe. To each type of atom is assigned a set of elementary states (eigenstates), each state corresponding to a different structure. It is these states, rather than the atoms themselves, that are the end-products of our analysis. The atom itself is a combination of its states; or, as we generally say, it has various probabilities of being in its different states. Similarly the ultimate structural unit (identified on p. 163 with a "simple existence symbol") is an electron or proton in an elementary state—not, as it is usually observed, in a combination of elementary states. When an atom is disturbed by other particles, its elementary states are not disturbed; their structure remains the same as when the atom is altogether isolated from its surroundings. The only thing disturbed is the distribution of probability between the various elementary states. Thus the analytical parts of the universe are self-sufficient as regards structure; but our observational knowledge is concerned with the distribution of probability among them, and in regard to the probability distribution they are interacting.

The more closely we study the method of quantum analysis, the more we appreciate the neatness of the way in which it overcomes the conflict of thought which requires the parts yielded by analysis to be conceptually independent, but interdependent in actual observation.

The fact that it is possible to analyse the universe into completely independent parts and then to add an interaction between the parts without in any way modifying the analysis, is less mysterious when we realise that an interaction can be wholly subjective. Even if the parts themselves are wholly objective, and have no physical influence on each other's behaviour, a subjective interaction may appear in our knowledge of them. We have seen that the end-products of our analysis must be identical structural units, which are therefore indistinguishable from each other observationally, so that they can be interchanged without affecting observation. Conversely the system inferable from observation—the knowable system—is less particularised than the objective system, for the individual particles in the knowable system are left unidentified. We can only say that a particle of the knowable system has equal probability of being any one of the objective particles. In comparing the behaviour of the knowable system with the behaviour of the objective system, account must be taken of the statistical effect of this indistinguishability. The effect is equivalent to that which would be produced by physical forces of interaction. For example, a particle may appear to deviate from its expected position because it has been acted on by a force or because, owing to the observational indistinguishability, another particle has been mistaken for it. An example of this purely subjective interaction was given on p. 36.

There is now strong reason to believe that *all* interaction forces in physics arise from the indistinguishability of the ultimate particles. Interaction has therefore a subjective origin. We have already conceded a partial subjectivity to the ultimate particles, but the interaction due to indistinguishability is independent of this. It is not an imperfection of our analysis that it fails to separate the universe into completely independent parts, and leaves a certain amount of interaction between them; it is rather the perfection of the analysis which brings about this result. We have already noticed (p. 97) that there is a kind of discontinuity between "good" and "perfect" in physics. "Perfect" is not so much the superlative of "good", as a "good" which has overreached itself and defeated its own aims. If the aim of analysis is to separate, it must stop short of the ultimate structural units; because when the parts become so simple that they are indistinguishable, their indistinguishability confuses them in our observational knowledge and, in a sense, undoes the separation which the analysis has effected.

V

"Substance" is one of the most dominant concepts in our familiar outlook on the world of sensory experience, and it is one with which science finds itself continually at war. We have already touched on one aspect of it—that it is essentially positive, as contrasted with form which is indifferently positive and negative. Another attribute of substance is its permanence or semi-permanence; and in this respect physics has rid itself of the concept of substance only to replace it by something equally permanent. Indirectly therefore substance still dominates our form of thought—a watered-down substance, of which no attribute survives but its permanence.

To accord with this form of thought, the analysis of the universe into parts is required to be, not a transitory partition, but a separation into parts which have some degree of permanence. Permanence is formulated scientifically in laws of conservation—conservation of mass, of energy, of momentum, of electric charge. In conjunction with the atomic concept, the requirement of permanence leads us to recognise, as the ultimate elementary particles, units (protons and electrons) which are normally, and probably altogether, indestructible. Further, in wave mechanics which deals explicitly with probability, we have an analysis into eigenstates, i.e. steady distributions of probability which have a considerable degree of permanence.

Owing to the difference of the natural time-scale concerned, permanence has a different epistemological significance in molar physics from permanence in microscopic physics. In the time-scale of atomic flux a hundredth of a second is virtually an eternity. A characteristic must be "everlasting" by this standard if it is to appear at all in the time-scale of ordinary human perception. There is therefore a clear reason for selecting the permanent and disregarding the transient features of microscopic systems. Classical, as well as modern, statistical mechanics is based on this consideration, which is probably the oldest epistemological principle explicitly accepted in physics. But permanence in molar physics refers to a much longer period of persistence, and there is not the same reason for concentrating attention on characteristics which possess it. That our subjective formulation of physical knowledge should impose a selection in favour of persistence up to a hundredth of a second or so is the natural result of the coarse-grainedness of our time-perception. If there is any selection in favour of persistence up to days and centuries, it must rest on other grounds.

I have emphasised the selective effect of the mind's insistence on permanence in my earlier writings, in which I was concerned only with molar physics.* It was the first hint of selective subjectivism that I came across. Looking back, I find it curious that I was first convinced of the subjective origin of some of the laws of nature by a consideration of molar law, and was inclined to regard the microscopic laws (at that time only dimly foreshadowed) as likely to be

* *Space, Time and Gravitation*, p. 196; *The Nature of the Physical World*, p. 241.

objective; because the application to molar law raises a difficult question which does not appear in the application to microscopic law. Let us consider this difference.

We regard the mind as demanding by its "necessities of thought" certain qualities in the parts which make up the physical universe. The mind imposes its demands by refusing to admit any system of analysis into parts which does not yield parts with the required qualities. The fundamental laws of physics are simply a mathematical formulation of the qualities of the parts into which our analysis has divided the universe; and it has been our contention that they are all imposed by the human mind in this way, and are therefore wholly subjective. It would be fatal to this view if it were found that the objective universe "plays up" to our analysis —that it exhibits an intrinsic tendency to separate into these parts, as though anticipating the mind's demand. We must therefore examine suspiciously any phenomena in which the parts seem spontaneously to present themselves separately, without having to be dug out by analysis.

In examining microscopic phenomena, we have to bear in mind the Procrustean methods of the experimenter which contrive to supply what our frame of thought demands. Like the sculptor, he renders visible the parts or combinations of parts which our analytical imagination creates; or at least his sorting and manufacturing operations produce effects which humour our belief that the parts are there. But in molar physics experimental interference is too limited to matter. Our apparatus cannot produce planets executing orbits prescribed to order in the way that it produces monochromatic light waves executing vibrations prescribed to order. If therefore we find in molar physics anything which seems to bolster up our adopted system of analysis, it threatens our theory more seriously.

The phenomenon requiring examination from this point of view is the presence of more or less permanent solid objects in the world of familiar apprehension. Although the persistence of material forms is not an exact equivalent of the scientific principle of conservation of mass, there is a fairly close association. Normally a considerable change of mass is associated with a perceptible change of material form. The permanent objects around us give, in a rough way, a continuous practical demonstration of the conservation of mass. This was scarcely to be expected; for *a priori* knowledge only forewarns us that the conservation of mass must occur, not that it will be shouted at us. There will be a conservation of something, but not necessarily of something apprehensible in sensation.

The world of familiar perception, consisting largely of objects with some degree of permanence, to this extent fits spontaneously into our form of thought. For this it seems an adequate explanation that without some degree of harmony between thought and sensation our continued existence would be impossible. To inquire how the harmony has come about —whether our sensory experience puts it into our heads to think as we do, or whether the evolution of man's senses has been guided by natural selection in such a way as not to conflict too grossly with his necessities of thought—may be like inquiring whether the hen comes first or the egg; and it is perhaps not very important to decide. We might well leave open the question whether the forms of thought which dominate our outlook are *acquired* or *innate*. But I am inclined to believe that the ultimate root is definitely mental— a predisposition inseparable from consciousness. It must be remembered that mere sensation does not determine what we ordinarily call the familiar world of sensory experience, in which the objects of more or less permanent form and size occur. That involves a combination of sense with commonsense. Of our various senses only sight and touch have any responsibility for the familiar conception of an external world of permanent solid objects. The primitive forms of sight and touch—a general sensitiveness to light and darkness, and a sensitiveness of flexible tentacles—provide little material for a concept of permanence. From these beginnings an elaborated sensory system has been evolved in such a way as to put vividly before us a world conformable to the mind's requirement of permanence.

It is clear that our sensory equipment must have a selective effect on the knowledge acquired through it. The form of thought which exhibits observational knowledge as a description of an external world, represents that world as containing nerves and brains through which observational knowledge is acquired by minds. The selection of the parts or combinations of parts of the universe to perform this function of transmission, determines the relative prominence of the various parts and combinations of parts in our sensory experience. It is the aim of physics to eliminate this adventitious prominence, so that ultimately it does not concern the scientific description of the universe; for example, the scientific description does not recognise any break between visible and ultra-violet radiation. But the prominence in our familiar outlook acquired by a part through its close relation to the mechanism of sensation has much the same effect in molar physics as the sorting out by experimental interference has in microscopic physics; either method of isolation gives the part a vividness in our experience which at first sight seems out of keeping with the view that it is merely the product of a conventional system of analysis.

I conclude that it is not necessarily a disproof of the *a priori* character of a physical law to find it closely illustrated by a prominent feature of the world of familiar apprehension. Familiar apprehension is subject to the same necessities of thought as those which, by more systematic application, yield the scientific description of the universe; so that a partial congruence is not unexpected.

VI

The following survey of our position emphasises more especially the point we have been considering in the last section:

(1) By consideration of certain deeply rooted forms of thought we can foresee the fundamental laws and constants which occur in the physical description of the universe, the description having been developed under the guidance of those forms of thought. But we cannot foresee what will be the correspondence between elements in this *a priori* physical description and elements in our familiar apprehension of the universe.

(2) The correspondence might be so remote that the *a priori* theory would seem almost irrelevant to observation. But actually the correspondence is fairly elementary. We do not have to search unduly far in our familiar experience before we come across the things which obey the laws prescribed by the *a priori* theory. We can almost see protons and electrons in a Wilson chamber; we can almost see mass being conserved. We do not actually see these things; but what we do see has a very close relation to them.

(3) We could force observational knowledge, whatever it might happen to be, into a predetermined frame of thought. The significance of (2) is that observational knowledge seems to show a predisposition to fit into the frame of thought without overmuch forcing. This predisposition, however, should not be exaggerated. The very wide rift now existing between the familiar world and the world described in modern scientific theories is a measure of the amount of forcing that has been found necessary.

(4) From this point of view "seeing" electrons and protons is not so significant as "seeing" conservation of mass. Electrons and protons are sorted out by experimental interference; but the perception of objects which illustrate

conservation of mass occurs without artificial conditions and is apparently a spontaneous testimony of sensation to the appropriateness of the *a priori* analysis.

(5) The existence of certain lines of sensory communication, relating sensations in consciousness to selected entities or conditions in the physical world, is a selective factor in our knowledge. This selection is altogether outside our present control, but it is conditioned by the fact that life would be impossible without some degree of harmony between the results of the selection and our engrained forms of thought. Consequently our perceptual recognition and abstraction of certain elements (permanent physical objects) out of the web of interconnectedness which makes up the physical universe follows with a rude approximation the same lines as the scientific analysis of the physical universe based on the same engrained forms of thought.

The primitive forms of thought which continue to dominate physics in spite of the modern revolution are:

(1) The form which formulates knowledge obtained through sensory experience as a description of a universe. It is through this that the physical universe is introduced and defined.

(2) The concept of analysis, which represents the universe as a coexistence of a number of parts. As used in physics the concept is not limited to "substance-analysis" which requires all the parts to be positive. In the more general conception of "form-analysis" the parts are indifferently positive and negative; and it is a consequence of this generality that the significance of a part cannot be detached from the system of analysis of which it is the result.

(3) The atomic concept, which requires the system of analysis to be such that the ultimate parts are identical structural units; so that all variety originates in the structure and not in the elements out of which the structure is built.

(4) The concept of permanence (a modified form of the concept of substance) which requires the ultimate parts to have some degree of permanence. This also leads us to give special recognition to permanent or semi-permanent combinations of parts, and to characteristics which remain permanent in the vicissitudes of phenomena.

(5) A concept of self-sufficiency of the parts (derived presumably from the concept of existence). This to some extent conflicts with the foregoing conceptions. By a compromise the parts are regarded as *intrinsically* self-sufficient, but interacting *in our knowledge* which is concerned with probability. This takes advantage of the irreversible relation between observation and formulated knowledge introduced by the probability concept (p. 91). We might, in fact, deduce the irreversibility (and hence the need for the probability concept) as an epistemological consequence of the frame of thought which requires the elementary physical systems to be isolable and yet observable.

This list may not be exhaustive, but it seems to embrace the forms chiefly responsible for our present outlook. It is important that they should be brought into the open, when we are considering how much physical science is determined by the *a priori* form of knowledge and how much by an objective source of that knowledge. Having, as far as we can, traced the primitive sources of the scientific frame of thought, we now turn to consider the frame which, by sophisticated intellectual effort, has been developed out of them. The frame described in the next chapter represents the present frontier of advance. Even the mathematical physicist does not maintain so advanced a level of thought habitually; and it is usual to return to more familiar modes of formulation to appreciate the fruits of the advance.

CHAPTER IX

THE CONCEPT OF STRUCTURE

I

THEORETICAL physics to-day is highly mathematical. Where does the mathematics come from? I cannot accept Jeans's view that mathematical conceptions appear in physics because it deals with a universe created by a Pure Mathematician; my opinion of pure mathematicians, though respectful, is not so exalted as that. An unbiased consideration of human experience as a whole does not suggest that either the experience itself or the truth revealed in it is of such a nature as to resolve itself spontaneously into mathematical conceptions. The mathematics is not there till we put it there. The question to be discussed in this chapter is, At what point does the mathematician contrive to get a grip on material which intrinsically does not seem particularly fitted for his manipulations?

The mathematician will naturally begin by introducing a number of symbols. Contrary to the popular belief, this does not of itself render a subject mathematical. If in a public lecture I use the common abbreviation *No.* for a number, nobody protests; but if I abbreviate it as *N*, it will be reported that "at this point the lecturer deviated into higher mathematics". Disregarding such prejudices, we must recognise that the allocation of symbols *A, B, C, ...* to various entities or qualities is merely an abbreviated nomenclature which involves no mathematical conceptions.

The next step is to introduce some kind of relation or comparison between *A* and *B*. If we examine the mental process of comparing two objects, I think we shall catch ourselves imagining a series of objects intermediate between them. We can best realise how they differ by considering what we should have to do to change one continuously into the other. If the idea of gradually modifying one into the other is too far-fetched, we simply decide that the two objects are so utterly unlike that a comparison would be meaningless. It will therefore be useful to introduce the conception of an operation which changes one object or quality into another. For example, the conception of an operation of expansion is useful when we have to compare objects of different size. Accordingly alongside our original A, B, C, ..., we have a new set of symbols P, Q, R, ..., standing for the operations which change A into B, A into C, B into C, etc.

But we are still in the stage of nomenclature, and mathematics seems as far off as ever. To continue, we must try to compare the operations P, Q, R, ... with one another. According to our former conclusion this leads us to imagine an operation of changing the operation P into the operation Q. Thus we have a new set of operations (or hyper-operations) X, Y, Z, ..., which change P into Q, P into R, Q into R, ... And so we go on in an orgy of notation, introducing more and more symbols, but never getting beyond notation.

It is easy to introduce mathematical notation; the difficulty is to turn it to useful account:

> Let x denote beauty, y manners well-bred,
> z fortune (this last is essential),
> Let L stand for love—our philosopher said—
> Then L is a function of x, y and z
>   Of the kind that is known as potential.
>
> Now integrate L with respect to dt
>   (t standing for time and persuasion)
> Then, between proper limits, 'tis easy to see
> The definite integral Marriage must be
>   (A very concise demonstration).*

* Prof. W. J. M. Rankine, *Songs and Fables*, 1874.

At the start there is no essential difference between this example of mathematical notation, and the A, B, C, ..., P, Q, R, ..., X, Y, Z, ..., that we have been discussing. We must find what it is that turns the latter into a powerful calculus for scientific purposes, whereas the former has no practical outcome—as the poem goes on to relate.

To introduce mathematics we must somehow put a stop to the infinite regression of symbols. Such a termination will be reached if we find that the X, Y, Z, ... are not new operations, but are already contained in the first set of operations P, Q, R, ... that we introduced; that is to say, if we find that the same operation which changes one entity into another will also change one operation into another.

As an example, consider the operations of duplicating, triplicating, quadruplicating, etc. If these are taken as P, Q, R, ..., we have next to consider, say, the operation Y which changes duplicating into quadruplicating. Quadruplication consists of two operations of duplication, i.e. of duplicating duplication. Thus the operation Y is *duplicating*, and has already been introduced as P. More generally if the set P, Q, R, ... denotes all possible operations of multiplication, fractional as well as integral, the operations of changing P into Q, P into R, Q into R, etc. are also operations of multiplication, and therefore no new symbols are required.

As another example, suppose that the initial entities A, B, C, ... are points on a sphere. The operation of changing one point on a sphere into another is a rotation of the sphere; thus the operations P, Q, R, ... are rotations. If P and Q are rotations through equal angles in different planes, the one plane is changed into the other, and therefore P into Q, by another rotation, say R. If P and Q are rotations through unequal angles, one can be changed into the other by a combination of the operations of rotation and multiplication. Grouping together all possible operations of rotation and multiplication, no further operations are introduced in comparing one rotation with another.

We see therefore that there exist "terminable sets of operations" which do not lead to a regression of nomenclature of ever-increasing complexity. It is only through such terminable sets that mathematical thought can be introduced. To the extent to which the various portions of our experience can be related to one another in terms of these operations they form material for mathematical treatment. The full development of the idea, here briefly indicated, is contained in the *Theory of Groups*.*

II

A terminable set of operations, or as it is technically called a *group*, has a structure which can be described mathematically. The fact that the operation which changes P into Q is always another member R of the group furnishes a set of triangular connections as the groundwork of the structure. These triangular connections can interlace in a great variety of patterns; and it is the pattern of the interlacing which constitutes the abstract structure. Groups are differentiated from one another by their abstract structure. The mathematical description of the group specifies only the pattern of interlacing, and pays no attention to the physical nature of the operations which yield this pattern. We may therefore have quite different sets of operations with the same group-structure, and therefore equivalent so far as mathematical description is concerned.

One of the most important groups in physics is the group of rotations in six dimensions. There are fifteen independent planes of rotation in six-dimensional space (corresponding to the three independent planes of rotation in three-dimensional

---

* An elementary account of the theory of groups, and of the part it plays in the foundations of theoretical physics, is given in *New Pathways in Science*, Ch. xii.

space); and since we have always to add the operation of "leaving things as they are", which is an *ex officio* member of every group, we have sixteen elements with which to form a group-structure. A definite interlocking pattern is constituted by the association of these elements (other than the *ex officio* element) in six sets of five (pentads), each element being a member of two pentads. Interlacing with it is an association of the elements in triads, the triads themselves being associated in conjugate pairs. Each of the fifteen elements plays an equivalent part in the pattern.

Rotation in six dimensions is only one of many sets of operations which yield this particular group-pattern. For example, if we place four different coins on the table, the operations of interchanging them in pairs, with or without turning one pair the other way up, form a group with this structure.* The same pattern of relations turns up in the geometry of Kummer's Quartic Surface, in the theory of Theta Functions, and—most important of all for our purposes—in the specification of an elementary particle (proton or electron) in an elementary state, including the specification of its charge and spin.

Properly to realise the conception of group-structure, we must think of the pattern of interweaving as abstracted altogether from the particular entities and relations that furnish the pattern. In particular, we can give an exact mathematical description of the pattern, although mathematics may be quite inappropriate to describe what we know of the nature of the entities and operations concerned in it. In this way mathematics gets a footing in knowledge which intrinsically is not of a kind suggesting mathematical conceptions. Its function is to elucidate the group-structure of the elements of that knowledge. It dismisses the individual elements by assigning to them symbols, leaving it to non-

* *New Pathways in Science*, p. 267. Letters are there substituted for coins.

mathematical thought to express the knowledge, if any, that we may have of what the symbols stand for.

We shall refer to this abstraction as the mathematical concept of structure, or briefly as the *concept of structure*. Since the structure, abstracted from whatever possesses the structure, can be exactly specified by mathematical formulae, our knowledge of structure is communicable, whereas much of our knowledge is incommunicable. I cannot convey to you the vivid knowledge which I have of my own sensations and emotions. There is no way of comparing my sensation of the taste of mutton with your sensation of the taste of mutton; I can only know what it tastes like to me, and you can only know what it tastes like to you. But if we are both looking at a landscape, although there is no way of comparing our visual sensations as such, we can compare the *structures* of our respective visual impressions of the landscape. It is possible for a group of sensations in my mind to have the same structure as a group of sensations in your mind. It is possible also that a group of entities which are not sensations in anyone's mind, associated together by relations of which we can form no conception, may have this same structure. We can therefore have structural knowledge of that which is outside everyone's mind. This knowledge will consist of the same kind of assertions as those which are made about the physical universe in the modern theories of mathematical physics. For strict expression of physical knowledge a mathematical form is essential, because that is the only way in which we can confine its assertions to structural knowledge. Every path to knowledge of what lies beneath the structure is then blocked by an impenetrable mathematical symbol.

Physical science consists of purely structural knowledge, so that we know only the structure of the universe which it describes. This is not a conjecture as to the nature of physical knowledge; it is precisely what physical knowledge as formulated in present-day theory states itself to be. In fundamental investigations the conception of group-structure appears quite explicitly as the starting point; and nowhere in the subsequent development do we admit material not derived from group-structure.

The fact that structural knowledge can be detached from knowledge of the entities forming the structure, gets over the difficulty of understanding how it is possible to conceive a knowledge of anything which is not part of our own minds. So long as the knowledge is confined to assertions of structure, it is not tied down to any particular realm of content. It will be remembered that we have separated the question of the nature of knowledge from the question of assurance of its truth. We are not here considering how it is possible to be assured of the truth of knowledge relating to something outside our minds; we are occupied with the prior question how it is possible to make any kind of assertion about things outside our minds, which (whether true or false) has a definable meaning.

III

I wonder if you hesitated before accepting my statement (p. 139) that quadruplicating is a duplicating of the operation of duplicating. If I had said "four times is twice twice" you would have admitted it unhesitatingly; but it suggests itself that duplicating or twicing as applied to an operation might well mean doing it over again for a check, and it is rather gratuitous to assume that the second operation is necessarily done on the end-product of the first.

Outside mathematics the statement that "two and two is four" is rather too sweeping; but we may go so far as to assert that, if "two and two" is a number at all, that number is four. In other words, if duplicating, triplicating, etc. are understood to form a group, i.e. a terminable set of operations, so that when applied to each other they yield other operations of the set, then the member of the set obtained by duplicating duplicating is quadruplicating.

Suppose, however, we accept the other meaning, so that when the operation of duplicating is applied to duplicating it yields a new kind of operation, different from any of the original set, which we may describe as a "checked duplication". Let us try another duplication. The twice performed multiplication by two is itself to be duplicated; and this can have no other meaning than that the multiplication by two is performed four times. Thus, if not at the first step, at any rate at the second step, we reach the group concept of duplicating which conforms to the rule that four times is twice twice. This is in accordance with what we have already noticed—that mathematical thought does not begin to take charge until the second step, when we reach relations between relations or operations on operations.

In order to formulate this point explicitly we shall distinguish between a *structural concept* and more general kinds of concept. A structural concept is obtained from a corresponding general concept by eliminating from our conception everything which is not essential to the part it plays in a group-structure. It is an element in a specified pattern without any properties except its connection with the pattern. Its properties are those of a mathematical symbol, which consist solely of its associations (or, more strictly the associations of its associations) with other symbols. The corresponding general concept, if any, is our conception of what the symbol represents in our ordinary non-mathematical form of thought. A general concept lacks the precision of a mathematical concept, and is often difficult to pin down to anything definite. Except as applied to sensations, emotions, etc. of which we can be directly aware, it is doubtful if the general concept is more than a self-deception which persuades us that we have an apprehension of something which we cannot apprehend. Nevertheless, such concepts must be reckoned with as part of our engrained form of thought.

The concepts referred to in Chapter VIII were general concepts occurring in our ordinary form of thought. It is now possible to add that in employing them to furnish the frame of thought in which our scientific knowledge is contained, we have gradually eliminated their general aspects, until now we recognise only the corresponding structural concepts. Correspondingly the resulting frame of thought has become a mathematical frame, and the knowledge contained in it is mathematical knowledge—a knowledge of group-structure. By introducing the mathematical theory of structure modern physics is able to carry out in a precise manner the general principles described in the last chapter. For example, we there insisted that the significance of a part cannot be dissociated from the system of analysis to which it belongs. As a structural concept the part is a symbol having no properties except as a constituent of the group-structure of a set of parts.

To show how these ideas are applied, let us consider the concept of *space*. Taking first the general concept, we usually regard infinite Euclidean space as the simplest kind of space to conceive. One would have thought that the infinitude would be rather a serious obstacle to conception; but most people manage to persuade themselves that they have overcome the difficulty, and even profess themselves utterly unable to conceive a space without infinitude. But, whatever the truth about the general concept, the structural concept of Euclidean space is exceptionally difficult. Since I want to give here a comparatively easy illustration, I will consider uniform spherical space which has a much simpler structural concept.

Any point in spherical space can be changed into any other point by a rotation of the sphere. Thus to the points or elements of spherical space, A, B, C, ..., there correspond operators P, Q, R, ... which are the rotations of the sphere; and the group of the operators is simply the group of rotations in the proper number of dimensions (in this case four dimensions). Regarding "space" as a structural concept, *all* that we know about spherical space is that it has the group-structure of this group of rotations. When we introduce spherical space in physics we refer to something—we know not what—which has this structure. Equally, if we refer to Euclidean space we refer to something—we know not what—with a specifiable group-structure, though it requires rather more advanced mathematical conceptions to formulate the specification. Similarly the space of irregular curvature which appears in Einstein's theory is something with a group-structure requiring rather more elaborate specification.

The general concept, which attempts to describe space as it appears in familiar apprehension—what it looks like, what it feels like, its negativeness as compared with matter, its "thereness"—is an embellishment of the bare structural description. So far as physical knowledge is concerned, this embellishment is an unauthorised addition. Philosophically it is all to the good if we find a difficulty in conceiving in non-mathematical forms of thought the kinds of space which modern physics has introduced; for we are thereby discouraged from making such embellishments.

IV

The mathematical theory of structure is the answer of modern physics to a question which has profoundly vexed philosophers.

But, if I never know directly events in the external world, but only their alleged effects on my brain, and if I never know my brain except in terms of its alleged effects on my brain, I can only reiterate in bewilderment my original questions: "What sort of thing is it that I know?" and "Where is it?"[*]

[*] C. E. M. Joad, *Aristotelian Society*, Supp. vol. IX, p. 137. Quoted by L. S. Stebbing, *Philosophy and the Physicists*, p. 64.

What sort of thing is it that I know? The answer is *structure*. To be quite precise, it is structure of the kind defined and investigated in the mathematical theory of groups.

It is right that the importance and difficulty of the question should be emphasised. But I think that many prominent philosophers, under the impression that they have set the physicists an insoluble conundrum, make it an excuse to turn their backs on the external world of physics and welter in a barren realism which is a negation of all that physical science has accomplished in unravelling the complexity of sensory experience. The mathematical physicist, however, welcomes the question as one falling especially within his province, in which his specialised knowledge may be of service to the general advancement of philosophy.

The phrase "if I never know my brain except in terms of its alleged effects on my brain" vividly, if not altogether accurately,* describes the conditions under which we labour. But it is not very alarming to the physicist, whose subject abounds with this kind of cyclic dependence. We only know an electric force by its effects on an electric charge; and we only know electric charges in terms of the electric forces they produce. It has long been evident that this is no bar to knowledge; but it is only recently that the systematic method of formulating such knowledge in terms of group-structure has become a recognised procedure in physical theory.

The bewilderment of the philosophers evidently arises from a belief that, if we start from zero, any knowledge of the external world must begin with the assumption that a sensation makes us aware of something in the external world —something differing from the sensation itself because it is non-mental. But knowledge of the physical universe does not begin in that way. One sensation (divorced from know-

* A more accurate form would be: "if I never know any brain except in terms of its alleged effects on a brain."

ledge already obtained by other sensations) tells us nothing; it does not even hint at anything outside the consciousness in which it occurs. The starting point* of physical science is knowledge of *the group-structure of a set of sensations* in a consciousness. When these fragments of structure, contributed at various times and by various individuals, have been collated and represented according to the forms of thought that we have discussed, and when the gaps have been filled by an inferred structure depending on the regularities discovered in the directly known portions, we obtain the structure known as the physical universe.

After this general synthesis of structure, we are in a position to describe any particular portion of the structure in the terms in which physical knowledge is ordinarily expressed. This will provide an alternative (physical) description of the original sensations. Since they are elements of a structure of sensations, and this structure has been incorporated in the structure which constitutes the physical universe, we can describe them in physical terms. Our physiological knowledge is probably insufficient to specify the exact physical event which is also a sensation in someone's mind; but approximately enough for most purposes we may take it to be a set of electrical impulses occurring at the brain-terminal of a bundle of nerves.

It is important to notice that the interpretation of sensory experience, like the interpretation of a cipher, includes two distinct problems. "Interpreting a cipher" may mean the procedure of discovering the code, or it may mean decoding a particular message with the code already known. In the same way, the procedure of interpreting our sensations as information about an external world may refer to the problem, which stands at the beginning of physics, of associating the fragments of structure in consciousness with

* I mean the logical starting point, not the historical starting point, of a subject which has grown out of crude beginnings.

the structure of an external universe; or it may refer to the particular information obtainable from each new sensation when we apply our accumulated physical and physiological knowledge. In regard to the initial problem, a single sensation is no more informative than a single letter in a cipher of which we have not the key. But, after the initial problem has been solved, we are able to interpret sensations individually as a cipher is decoded letter by letter. A sensation of noise informs me of an electrical disturbance of a particular nerve-terminal—which, of course, does not mean that it informs me that this is the correct physical description of what has occurred. The description is provided beforehand by the solution of the initial problem, so that it is ready for use when the sensation informs me that an event has occurred to which it is applicable.

The disturbance at the nerve terminal is generally the result of a long chain of causation in the physical world. In familiar thought we usually leap to the far end of the chain of causation, and say that the sensation is caused by an object at some distance from the seat of the sensation. In the case of the visual sensation caused by a spiral nebula, the object is not only remote in space but may be millions of years distant in time. Causation bridges the gap in space and time, but the physical event at the seat of sensation (provisionally identified with an electrical disturbance of a nerve terminal) is not the *cause* of the sensation; it *is* the sensation. More precisely, the physical event is the structural concept of that of which the sensation is the general concept.

Thus, when you tell me that you hear a noise, the information imparted is represented in my knowledge by (*a*) a general concept of a heard-noise, i.e. a concept of something of similar nature to my own awareness of noises, and (*b*) a structural concept of a heard-noise, i.e. a part of the structure of the physical universe which we describe as an electrically disturbed terminal of an auditory nerve. Of these two concepts of a heard-noise, the one refers to what it is in itself, the other refers to what it is as a constituent of the structure known as the physical universe.

V

The recognition that physical knowledge is structural knowledge abolishes all dualism of consciousness and matter. Dualism depends on the belief that we find in the external world something of a nature incommensurable with what we find in consciousness; but all that physical science reveals to us in the external world is group-structure, and group-structure is also to be found in consciousness. When we take a structure of sensations in a particular consciousness and describe it in physical terms as part of the structure of an external world, it is still a structure of sensations. It would be entirely pointless to invent something else for it to be a structure of. Or, to put it another way, there is no point in inventing non-physical replicas of certain portions of the structure of the external world and transferring to the replicas the non-structural qualities of which we are aware in sensation. The portions of the external universe of which we have additional knowledge by direct awareness amount to a very small fraction of the whole; of the rest we know only the structure, and not what it is a structure of.

Let us denote by X the entity of which the physical universe is the structure,* and distinguish the small part X_s known to be of sensory nature from the remainder X_u of which we have no direct awareness. It may be suggested that there remains a dualism of X_s and X_u equivalent to the old dualism of consciousness and matter; but this is, I think, a logical confusion, involving a switch over from the epistemological view of the universe as the theme of knowledge

---

* I usually call X the "external world", the "physical world" being limited to the structure of the external world.

to an existential view of the universe as something of which we have to obtain knowledge. Structurally X_u is no different from X_s, and to give meaning to the supposed dualism we have to imagine a supplementary non-structural knowledge of X_u revealing its unlikeness to X_s. We have to suppose that a direct awareness of X_u, if we could possess it, would show that it was not of sensory nature. But the supposition is nonsense; for if we had the supposed direct awareness of X_u, it would *ipso facto* be a sensation in our consciousness. Thus we cannot give meaning to the dualism without making a supposition which eliminates the dualism.

Although the statement that the universe is of the nature of "a thought or sensation in a universal Mind" is open to criticism, it does at least avoid this logical confusion. It is, I think, true in the sense that it is a logical consequence of the form of thought which formulates our knowledge as a description of a universe. But it requires more guarded expression if it is to be accepted as a truth transcending forms of thought.

To sum up. The physical universe is a structure. Of the X of which it is the structure, we only know that X includes sensations in consciousness. To the question : What is X when it is not a sensation in any consciousness known to us? the right answer is probably that the question is a meaningless one—that a structure does not necessarily imply an X of which it is the structure. In other words, the question takes us to a point where the form of thought in which it originates ceases to be useful. The form of thought can only be preserved by still attributing to X a sensory nature—a sensation in a consciousness unknown to us. What interests us is not the positive conclusion, but the fact that in no circumstances are we required to contemplate an X of non-sensory nature.

The fact that the concept of structure affords an escape from dualism has been recognised especially in the philosophy of Bertrand Russell. Although I have quoted it in three earlier books, I feel obliged to quote again a passage from Russell's *Introduction to Mathematical Philosophy* (1919) which has greatly influenced my own thought:

"There has been a great deal of speculation in traditional philosophy which might have been avoided if the importance of structure, and the difficulty of getting behind it, had been realised. For example, it is often said that space and time are subjective, but they have objective counterparts; or that phenomena are subjective, but are caused by things in themselves, which must have differences *inter se* corresponding with the differences in the phenomena to which they give rise. Where such hypotheses are made, it is generally supposed that we can know very little about the objective counterparts. In actual fact, however, if the hypotheses as stated were correct, the objective counterparts would form a world having the same structure as the phenomenal world....In short, every proposition having a communicable significance must be true of both worlds or of neither; the only difference must lie in just that essence of individuality which always eludes words and baffles description, but which for that very reason is irrelevant to science."

This was written independently of the new scientific theories, which were then in an early stage; but it illuminated the philosophic trend which was beginning to appear in them. It is interesting to compare the scientific position in 1919 with the position in 1939. In 1919 it was a fair inference that physical knowledge must be knowledge of structure, although in the form in which it was then presented it did not look much like it. In general the structural knowledge did not appear in physics explicitly; it was thought of as the kernel of truth which would outlast the changing theories which enhulled it. In the intervening years the importance of digging out the structure from its inessential trappings became recognised, and it was noticed that in the Theory of

Groups in pure mathematics the necessary technique had been developed. Moreover, the idea of structure, which had previously been rather vague, was found capable of exact mathematical definition. Consequently to-day it is not merely a truth hidden in our physical knowledge but physical knowledge in its current form that we recognise as structural.

CHAPTER X

THE CONCEPT OF EXISTENCE

I

I FIND a difficulty in understanding books on philosophy because they talk a great deal about "existence", and I do not know what they mean. Existence seems to be a rather important property, because I gather that one of the main sources of division between different schools of philosophy is the question whether certain things exist or not. But I cannot even begin to understand these issues, because I can find no explanation of the term "exist".

The word "existence" is, of course, familiar in everyday speech; but it does not express a uniform idea—a universally agreed principle according to which things can be divided into existing and non-existing. Difference of opinion as to whether a thing exists or not sometimes arises because the thing itself is imperfectly defined, or because the exact implications of the definition have not been grasped; thus the "real existence" of electrons, aether, space, colour, may be affirmed or denied because different persons use these terms with somewhat different implications. But ambiguity of definition is not always responsible for the difference of view. Let us take something familiar, say an overdraft at a bank. No one can fail to understand precisely what that means. Is an overdraft something which exists? If the question were put to the vote, I think some would say that its existence must be accepted as a grim reality, and others would consider it illogical to concede existence to what is intrinsically a negation. But what divides the two parties is no more than a question of words. It would be absurd to divide mankind into two sects, the one believing in the existence of overdrafts and the other denying their existence. The division is a question of classification, not of belief. If you tell me your own answer, I shall not learn anything new about the nature or properties of an overdraft; but I shall learn something about your usage of the term "exists"—what category of things you intend it to cover.

It is a primitive form of thought that things either exist or do not exist; and the concept of a category of things possessing existence results from forcing our knowledge into a corresponding frame of thought. Everyone does this instinctively; but there are borderline cases in which all do not employ the same criteria, as the example of the overdraft shows. A philosopher is not bound by traditional or instinctive conventions to the same extent as a layman; and when he similarly expresses his knowledge in this primitive frame of thought, it is impossible to guess what classificatory system he will adopt. It would be rather surprising if all philosophers adopted the same system. In any case I do not see why such a mystery should be made of it, nor how an arbitrary decision as to the classification to be adopted has come to be transformed into a fervid philosophical belief.

I do not want to make sweeping charges on the basis of a very limited reading of philosophy. I am aware that in the more recondite works the meaning of the term is sometimes discussed. But, after all, philosophers do occasionally write for the layman; and some of them seek to repel the scientific invader in language which he is supposed to understand. What I complain of is that these writers do not seem to realise that the term "exist", if they do not explain the meaning *they* attach to it, must necessarily be as bewildering to the scientist, as, for example, the term "curvature of space", if left unexplained, would be to the philosopher. And I think it is not an unfair inference from this omission that they themselves attach more importance to the word than to its meaning.

It is not every sentence containing the verb "to exist" that troubles me. The term is often used in an intelligible way. For me (and, it appears, also for my dictionary) "exists" is a rather emphatic form of "is". "A thought exists in somebody's mind," i.e. a thought is in somebody's mind—I can understand that. "A state of war exists in Ruritania," i.e. a state of war is in Ruritania—not very good English, but intelligible. But when a philosopher says "Familiar chairs and tables exist", i.e. familiar chairs and tables are..., I wait for him to conclude. Yes? What were you going to say they are? But he never finishes the sentence. Philosophy seems to me full of half-finished sentences; and I do not know what to make of it.

Speech is often elliptical, and I do not mind unfinished sentences if I know how they are meant to be finished. "A horrible noise exists" presumably is intended to be completed in some such form as "A horrible noise is—disturbing me". But that is not how the philosopher intends me to complete his unfinished statement "noises actually exist"—and I really have no idea what completion he does intend. I myself, when I am not intimidated by the existence* of critics determined to make nonsense of my words if it is possible to do so, often say that atoms and electrons exist. I mean, of course, that they exist—or are—in the physical world, that being the theme of discussion in the context. We need not examine the precise ellipsis by which a mathematician says that the root of an equation exists, when he means that the equation has a root; it is sufficient to say that he has no idea of putting forward a claim to include the root of a mathematical equation in the category of things which philosophers speak of as "really existing".

In the preceding chapters I have discussed a number of

* No; you have not caught me this time. The critics intimidate me just as much, whether philosophy concedes to them "real existence" or not.

things which exist in the physical universe; that is to say, they are in, or are parts of, the physical universe. We have seen that "to exist in", even in the equivalent expression "to be part of", is not free from ambiguity, and is made definite only by the conventions discussed in connection with the concept of analysis. The question whether the physical universe itself exists has not arisen. I have, in fact, avoided saying that it exists—which would be an unfinished sentence. Ordinarily it would be unnecessary to be so particular. The existence or non-existence of things is a primitive form of thought; and, if I had used the term, it would mean no more than that I was forcing our observational knowledge into such a frame,* as it is forced into several other frames that we have discussed. Knowing, however, that as philosophers we must seek to get behind these forms of thought, I have thought it best in this book to avoid introducing it even temporarily.

II

It is an advantage of the epistemological approach that the question of attributing a mysterious property called "existence" to the physical universe never arises. Let me remind you again of the position. Our starting point is a particular body of knowledge. We have no need to define knowledge —to discuss the exact scope of the term. What is required is a specification of the particular collection of knowledge or alleged knowledge which is to be the theme of discussion. Broadly this is taken to be whatever is received as knowledge within the domain of physical science according to the most up-to-date conclusions. In accordance with a supposed necessity of thought this knowledge has been formulated as a description of a physical universe. That is how the physical universe comes into the discussion. That, I think, is all that

* If we wish the assertion to mean more than the expression of a primitive form of thought, we say "really exists".

is needed to tell you just what the physical universe is; and you would not know any more about it if I added the unfinished sentence "the physical universe is an entity which is...", or even if I were so heterodox as to say "the physical universe is an entity which isn't...".

I have referred also to an objective universe which cannot be identified with the universe of which the above-mentioned body of knowledge forms a description. The latter universe is, as we have seen, partially subjective and partially objective. Some will perhaps say that until recently "physical universe" was always understood to mean the objective universe, and the term should still be used in that sense. It would then be necessary to draw a distinction between the physical universe and the universe of physics, i.e. the universe described in physics. When a term has been associated with several conceptions which are found to be conflicting, it is always a moot point which of them should have defining force. Doubtless the term "physical universe" was formerly intended to refer to something which possesses, along with other characteristics, pure objectivity; but to test whether *objectivity* is part of its definition, I must ask, "Will you stick to this definition whatever happens?" Suppose, for example, it should turn out that there is nothing purely objective in experience except God; will you agree that when you said "physical universe" you were really all the time referring to "God"? I do not think you will. But that means that the ultimate definition, which you are prepared to adhere to in all circumstances, is determined by other considerations. Objectivity is not a defining property, but a property which we had (wrongly, as it happens) expected the thing defined by other properties to possess. That being so, we must examine open-mindedly whether the physical universe possesses objectivity, and not try to smuggle in the objectivity as part of its definition.

Having rejected a definition postulating objectivity, we

come back to the epistemological definition that I have been following. The physical universe is the world which physical knowledge is formulated to describe; and there is no difference between the physical universe and the universe of physics.

It would be a serious objection to this definition if it could be said that it involves using the term in a sense different from that in which it is used in ordinary speech. Ordinary speech does not concern itself much with the universe; but the same consideration applies to parts of the universe, namely physical objects. Does the scientist mean by a "physical object" what the plain man would take it to mean? For example, when we give a scientific description of a chair according to the most modern physical theories, are we describing the object which in everyday life is called a chair?

Some of the pure philosophers deny that the scientific description applies to the objects which in ordinary speech are called physical objects. Their opinion is voiced by Prof. Stebbing: "He [the physicist] has never been concerned with *chairs*, and it lies beyond his competence to inform us that the chairs we sit upon are abstract."* Physicists are not concerned with chairs! Are we really expected to take this sitting down?

Let us first notice that the phrase "chairs we sit upon" adds nothing to the term "chair". For what sits on the chair is the body; and if we have to discriminate the scientific chair, i.e. the object, not really a chair, which the physicist describes, from the familiar chair, we must also discriminate the scientific body, i.e. the object, not really a body, which the physicist describes, from the familiar body. So when we sit on a chair, the familiar body sits on a familiar chair, and the scientific body sits on a scientific chair. And if there is an abstract body it doubtless performs an abstraction of sitting on an abstract chair.

I do not object to the philosopher contemplating a construct of sensory qualities which is not to be identified with

* L. S. Stebbing, *Philosophy and the Physicists*, p. 278.

the object described in physics. But when he claims that it is this philosophical chair and not the scientific chair that the ordinary man refers to, he is self-deceived. For if he were right, why is it that a Transport Company, wishing to improve its arrangements for seating, consults a physicist who is not concerned with the chairs we sit upon, instead of a philosopher who is?

If the physicist is not concerned with chairs, the astrophysicist is not concerned with stars. There is one Professor of Astrophysics, Prof. Dingle, who has not been afraid to recognise this logical conclusion: "He [Bertrand Russell] has missed the essential point that physics is not concerned at all with planets."* Prof. Dingle, like Prof. Stebbing, has dropped the outlook which determines the familiar use of words, and has strayed into a world where men look at things in the way philosophers would have them look, and language is diverted to describe those things which philosophers consider most worth attention.

> Twinkle, twinkle little star,
> How I wonder what you are!

But the child is not wondering whether the star is "a function of sense data" (Russell) or "a commonsense grouping of experiences" (Dingle). He is wondering how big it is and how far away, what keeps it from dropping down, whether it is made of gold, whether it is lit by electricity. When he wonders what a star is, it is Dingle the astrophysicist, not Dingle the philosopher, who can give him the information for which he thirsts. One question leads on to another; and in the recondite treatises of physics we are still asking, and now and again answering, the unceasing flow of questions. When a physicist tells us by his scientific description what a star is, he is still answering the child's question; but the child is a little older.

* H. Dingle, *Through Science to Philosophy*, p. 93.

It is true that the child—or the ordinary man—does not know that what he is really wondering about is the group structure of the star. But when we dole out to him bit by bit, in language adapted to the stage he has reached, particulars about the group structure, he recognises that the information is an answer to his half-formed questions. And his curiosity is not satisfied until he has extracted in this way everything we can tell him about the group structure, or until he finds we have become so unintelligible that it is useless to question us any longer.

The physicist himself may be partly to blame for the suspicion that he is talking about something different from what the ordinary man would mean by the physical universe and physical objects; for he has not always been scrupulous in his appropriation of familiar words. But there has been no misappropriation in this case.

The physical universe as described in this book may seem remote from the universe ordinarily contemplated because of the emphasis that has been laid on its subjectivity. But the suspicion that the term is being misused arises from a misunderstanding. It has been my special task in these lectures to study the subjective element in the physical universe, so that the objective element has been kept out of the limelight; but, as I have pointed out, the objective element bulks largely in the unsystematised part of our knowledge which also forms part of the description of the physical universe. When we put off the blinkers of the specialist, and view the two elements together in proper perspective, we shall find that they form a universe not unacceptable as an answer to the elementary questions which arise out of familiar experience, as well as to the more recondite scientific questions.

III

I hope it is now sufficiently clear that I repudiate any metaphysical concept of "real existence"; and I may without danger introduce a *structural concept of existence* which has a mathematically defined sense. It is a primitive form of thought that things either exist or do not exist. I suppose that everyone catches himself thinking that way, though he would find it impossible to crystallise the conception of existence referred to. Let us set aside the hazy general concept, and consider only the structure of the concept. Its very simple structure is represented by a symbol which contains in itself two possibilities—existence and non-existence. In mathematical language it is a symbol J with two eigenvalues, which are most conveniently taken to be 1, standing for existence, and 0, standing for non-existence. The symbol J must satisfy the equation $J^2 - J = 0$, since that is a quadratic equation which has just the two solutions $J = 1$ and $J = 0$. Another way of writing the same equation is $J^2 = J$. We call a symbol which is equal to its own square an *idempotent* symbol.

The structural concept of existence is represented by an idempotent symbol.

In general it requires more than one element to form a structure; and existence is the only example of a structure possessed by a single element. It will be remembered that structure first appears when the operation X which turns the operation P into the operation Q is not a new kind of operation but one of the set of operations already defined. When there is only one operation J to consider, this condition for structure degenerates into "the operation which turns the operation J into the operation J is the operation J". That is what the idempotent condition $J . J = J$ asserts. Thus, if we represent the ultimate elements of our analysis by idempotent symbols, we express the form of thought that, apart from its structural association with other elements, all that can be said about an element is that it exists, or alternatively that it does not exist.

The entity represented by the simple existence symbol J is like a point in that it "has no parts and no magnitude"; for if it had parts, it would be possible to conceive one part existing without the other, and each part would require an independent existence symbol. The existence of the whole, being equivalent to the co-existence of the parts, would then depend on a combination of their separate existence symbols, and not on a simple symbol J. The entity in physics which, like the point in pure geometry, has no parts is described as an *elementary particle*. At present our elementary particle has "no magnitude"; since magnitude is relative and we have introduced nothing to relate it to. The magnitudes (mass m, charge e, and range in nuclear phenomena) which we attribute to an elementary particle belong to it, not intrinsically, but on account of its relations to the rest of the universe.

Observation can only disclose the relations between entities; and the most elementary relation we can consider is the relation between two elementary particles with simple existence symbols J_1 and J_2, respectively. This relation only exists if both the particles exist. We therefore assign to it the double existence symbol $J_1 \times J_2$, which will have the existence eigenvalue 1 if both J_1 and J_2 have the eigenvalue 1, and the non-existence eigenvalue 0 if either or both have the eigenvalue 0.

A relation between two relations will exist only if both relations exist, and it should accordingly be assigned a quadruple existence symbol. But that way leads to an orgy of ever-expanding notation.* Our goal is a structure in which the relations of relations are represented by the same set of

* Quadruple existence symbols are however important at a later stage because a *measurement* involves four entities (p. 168).

symbols as the relations themselves, so that the conditions for a mathematical description in terms of group theory are fulfilled. The relations of relations will therefore have the double existence symbols of the simple relations with which they are identified.

It is to be remembered that the elementary particles are not actual data. The datum is our observational knowledge, which, since it is of communicable character, is necessarily a knowledge of group structure; and the elementary particle is a product of analysis of this group structure. The constituents of the group are the operators which we have called $P, Q, R \ldots$. We want now to express symbolically the fact that P, Q, R are *relations*. The structural concept of a relation is that it is something whose existence is contingent on the existence of two entities either of which could exist or not exist. Thus, in representing $P, Q, R \ldots$ by double existence symbols, we are saying no more about them than is necessary in order that they may be conceived as relations. Hitherto we have talked vaguely about a group structure of $P, Q, R\ldots$, but we can now specify the particular mathematical group involved, namely the group of the double existence symbols. On investigation this is found to be the same group as the group of rotations in six-dimensional space, to which reference has already been made (p. 140).

Why six dimensions? Even if we include time, the continuum of location revealed in observational experience has only four dimensions. But we are dealing with particles, not geometrical points; and the double existence symbol represents a relation between two particles more complex than (but including) the purely geometrical relation between the two points that they occupy. Not only is the greater complexity directly predicted by this method, but further development of the theory shows how it will manifest itself in observational experience. The additional complication corresponds to the plane of spin and sign of charge of an elementary particle— which have no counterparts in a geometrical point.

The next step in the theoretical development is conditioned by the fact that the elements of structure in the universe are exceedingly numerous. We have been contemplating a structure which does not "exist" unless every one of its elements exists. But, when the number of elements is very large, we have a somewhat different conception of the existence of the structure, according to which the presence of two or three elements more or less is not worth troubling about. Since no one of its particles is now essential to the existence of the structure, we must give the structure an existence symbol independent of the existence symbols of its individual particles.

To express this change of our form of thought, it must be noticed that it duplicates the existence of each element; as a contributor to the structure it is conceived to exist continually, but as an independent entity it may or may not be present. Let us express mathematically the nature of the *independent* existence that we attribute to it. We must first duplicate its ordinary existence symbol, obtaining $2J$. We then abstract the part which represents its existence as a contributor to the structure; this is not a potentiality of existence or non-existence for which symbolic representation is required, but unconditional existence which we have agreed to represent by the number 1. The remainder $2J-1$ represents the independent existence of the element. We thus obtain the conception of an independently existing particle, represented by an *independent existence symbol* $K = 2J - 1$. The eigenvalues of K are 1 for existence and -1 for non-existence. The absence of the particle is now, not a mere negation (0), but a hole (-1) occurring in, or added to, the structure.

Apart from its existence or non-existence, the only characteristic possessed by the elementary particle is its relation to the whole structure. In our new point of view the relation comes first. That is to say, we classify the different possible relations of an individual particle to the whole structure, and then to each possible relation we assign an independent existence symbol K which indicates whether a particle having that relation exists or not. The more usual terminology is to call the relation to the whole structure a *state*, and to describe the state as *occupied* or *unoccupied*. We may therefore call K an *occupation symbol* instead of an independent existence symbol.

In this mode of representation the "whole structure" plays a similar part to the geoid in geodesy, from which the actual earth is obtained by adding or subtracting material at various points. Having regard to this analogy I propose to call the structure that is contemplated as continually existing, the *uranoid*. This will distinguish it from other structures we may have occasion to consider. Each independent particle is independent only because it has contributed half its "existence" to the uranoid. This implies that the number of particles contemplated (but not necessarily existing) has been fixed at the start, and the uranoid constructed accordingly. We shall consider later how this number is determined.

IV

For the further steps in the development of theoretical physics from this epistemological foundation reference must be made to my mathematical treatise.* I have tried here, firstly to exhibit in detail the principles by which mathematics first gets a grip on the subject, so that we may understand the exact relation of the symbolic mathematical frame of thought to our non-mathematical conception of things; and secondly to carry the development far enough to show

* *Relativity Theory of Protons and Electrons* (1936), especially Chapter

that the mathematical material obtained in this way is not trivial. Neither at this stage nor at a later stage is there anything arbitrary in the course of the development, provided we admit that it must be such as to express knowledge according to certain forms of thought which we recognise as engrained in our outlook.

I must, however, mention a conception which arises in later developments, because there will be occasion to use it in the next chapter. Every state is ideally distinct, and is associated with a different symbol K which can denote only occupation or non-occupation; but in practice we sometimes ignore the more minute distinctions and run a great number of states into one. Thus we often have to do with condensed states, formed by running together n elementary states, and capable therefore of being occupied by any number up to n particles. To describe the state of occupation of a condensed state we must associate with it a *cardinal symbol K'*, whose eigenvalues are the integers from $-\tfrac{1}{2}n$ to $+\tfrac{1}{2}n$ and represent the excess of the number of occupied states over $\tfrac{1}{2}n$.* The equation satisfied by K' is

$$K'\left(1-K'^2\right)\left(1-K'^2/2^2\right)\left(1-K'^2/3^2\right)\ldots\left(1-K'^2/\tfrac{1}{4}n^2\right)=0$$

since its roots are the required eigenvalues. Usually n is so large that it is considered infinite, and the left-hand side of the equation is then an infinite product which is well known to be equal to $\sin \pi K'$. Thus the characteristic equation† of K' is $\sin \pi K' = 0$, which is satisfied by every integer, positive and negative, including zero. This is the form in which the equation is used in current quantum theory; but it is to be remembered that it is an approximation, and in the strict form of the equation there is a highest integer.

---

* We have taken n even. Appropriate modifications are introduced if n is odd. Half the existence of each particle, i.e. $\tfrac{1}{2}n$ altogether, is regarded as included in the uranoid, and the excess over $\tfrac{1}{2}n$ is therefore the independent existence associated with the condensed state.

† In the same sense in which $J^2 = J$ is the characteristic equation of J.

We shall gain some idea of the magnitude of the work that remains before the present development of theory on a purely epistemological basis merges into current physical theory, if we realise that we have not yet introduced *measurement*; so that the ordinary physical quantities which result from measurement have not yet appeared. In Chapter v we spent much time over the definitions of length and time interval which are the basis of all other physical measurements. This system of expression of our knowledge by measured physical quantities has yet to be linked on to the more primitive expression in terms of group structure.

We are said to "observe" a relation between two entities; but a "measurement" consists in comparing such a relation with a standard. Thus a measurement of length is a comparison of a relation of extension between two entities in the system under observation with a relation of extension between two entities marking the ends of our adopted standard. A measure therefore involves four entities, and at its first appearance is associated with a quadruple existence symbol. It is, however, conceptually transferred to the relation that is compared with the standard; and some measures (e.g. a measure of mass) are even transferred to a single entity chosen from the four. The formal treatment of this transference leads to very extensive ramifications of physical theory. Here we shall only note that the quadruple existence symbols, from which we turned aside near the beginning of this discussion, play an important part in the later stages because of their direct association with the process of measurement. This, however, is not the beginning of an infinite regression. The conceptual frame in which physical knowledge is expressed is such as to involve simple, double and quadruple existence symbols corresponding respectively to entities, relations and measures; but it has no fundamental use for octuple and higher symbols.

From the association of measurement with four entities

we are led, without further investigation, to expect that the number 4 will in some way make itself evident in the world-picture which embodies the results of our measurements. It is the seed from which spring those oddly assorted pure numbers which we call constants of nature (p. 58). This conclusion in itself tells us very little, and gives no warrant for numerological speculations. I believe that the number 4 introduced in this way is actually responsible for the four dimensions of space-time, *but only indirectly*. In an actual calculation the number of dimensions of space-time is reached by the route

$$\frac{4 \cdot 3}{1 \cdot 2} - 1 - 1 = 4,$$

and it is a coincidence that the number we end with is the number we start with. Many threads must be woven together before we make anything out of this small beginning.

One cannot make bricks without straw. The foregoing discussion will perhaps serve to show where I get the straw for the bricks which I make—or drop—in the complete theory.

CHAPTER XI

THE PHYSICAL UNIVERSE

I

I BELIEVE there are 15,747,724,136,275,002,577,605,653,961, 181,555,468,044,717,914,527,116,709,366,231,425,076,185, 631,031,296 protons in the universe, and the same number of electrons.

In this total a positron is counted as minus one electron; so that the creation and annihilation of electrons and positrons in pairs, which is continually happening, does not affect the total. How mesotrons are to be counted (if at all) in the total cannot be stated until we know more about these particles. Neutrons and nuclei are, of course, counted according to the number of protons and electrons composing them.

It ought not to be necessary to re-state what has been well known since 1920, that each nucleus is composed of a definite number of protons and electrons ascertainable from its atomic weight and atomic number. But a few years ago there was a craze for denying this, which spread so widely that the most harmless reference to it still evokes criticism— as though it betrayed ignorance of recent ideas of nuclear structure. The statement refers to the composition, not the structure, of the nucleus. Only those possessed of a singularly naïve imagination could ever have supposed it meant that a close inspection of the nucleus would reveal electrons sticking in it like currants in a pudding. A nucleus is composed of protons and electrons in the same way that an omelette is composed of eggs; that is to say, when the omelette appears on the table, there are fewer eggs in the larder. The proton-electron composition assigned to the various nuclei is amply confirmed by transmutation experiments which apply directly the "omelette" criterion of composition. I think the craze for a metaphysical pronouncement, that eggs and electrons cease to exist when they are scrambled, has now died away; but it was in any case an irrelevancy.

Coming back to the number of protons and electrons, I have stated my belief. One believes with varying degrees of confidence. My belief that I know the exact number of protons and electrons in the universe does not rank among my strongest scientific convictions, but I should describe it as a fair average sort of belief. I am, however, strongly convinced that, if I have got the number wrong, it is just a silly mistake, which would speedily be corrected if there were more workers in this field. In short, to know the exact number of particles in the universe is a perfectly legitimate aspiration of the physicist.

Cynical persons will say that it is rather a safe calculation, because no one will ever count the particles and show that my reckoning is, say, 14 out. I am going so far to justify the cynics as to admit that, if I had thought there was the least chance that anyone would count the particles, I would never have published my calculation. But my reason is not the one you suspect. The reason is that in the calculation I employed a type of analysis appropriate only to *uncountable* particles; so that if anyone persuaded me that he could actually count the protons and electrons, he would persuade me that my calculation was on a wrong basis, and I should withdraw it without waiting to hear whether his count disagreed.

Let us see why protons and electrons are uncountable. It is not merely because there are so many of them. Quantum physicists tell us that an electron is not definitely in one place but is smeared over a probability distribution; also that electrons are indistinguishable from one another. That is not very promising material for counting. There is nothing to remember about the electron you last counted—neither its position nor any distinguishing mark. So how can you know whether the next you notice is a new one or one already counted? By the uncertainty principle, the more closely you pin down its position at one instant, the more uncertain you are of its velocity and where it will turn up next. When you retire to rest, as a variant to counting sheep in a green field, perhaps you may like to try counting electrons in a probability distribution.

The nature of electrons makes it impossible to count them except in very special cases; and the same applies to protons. Nevertheless, physicists tell us confidently the approximate number of electrons (about $6 . 10^{23}$) in a gram of hydrogen. Obviously they have not counted them. That in itself does not call for criticism, because we recognise that it is legitimate to obtain such a result in an indirect way. Bankers determine (or used to determine) the number of sovereigns by weighing, knowing that this would give the same result as the more laborious process of counting. But can it be said that the indirect procedure used by physicists to determine the number of electrons in a gram of hydrogen gives the same result as would be obtained by actually counting them? Clearly not; because we have just seen that they cannot be counted— actually counting them would have given no result at all.

Every item of physical knowledge is an assertion of the result of an observational procedure actual or hypothetical. When knowledge is claimed of the number of protons and electrons in a gram of hydrogen, the observational procedure referred to cannot be counting. It must be knowledge of the result of some other procedure by which an integral number is affixed to a system. We call this number the number of particles; but it is the number reckoned according to a "quantum arithmetic" not based on the same conceptions as the Pythagorean arithmetic of counting.

Perhaps we ought to be angry with the quantum physicist for deluding us. But it is impossible not to admire the devastating beauty of quantum arithmetic, and the ingenuity of the trick by which it assigns number to the uncountable.

The name "arithmetic", like "geometry" or even "hydrodynamics", may be applied to a branch of pure mathematics with its own definitions and axioms unconnected with anything in the physical universe; but in scientific context these terms are to be understood in their original practical meaning as sciences having for their subject matter the numbering of physical objects, the measurement of the world and the movement of material fluids. As branches of physical science they are embraced in the general trend towards unification; and as relativity theory has unified geometry and mechanics, so quantum theory has even more audaciously unified arithmetic and wave mechanics. We have already seen (p. 75) that it is necessary to turn to quantum theory for a specification of the material standard of length by pure numbers only. Relativity theory is able to express knowledge in terms of number, but only because it has borrowed its standard of length from quantum theory, and with it the quantum association of numbers with physical systems.

The key to the unification which has turned arithmetic into wave mechanics is the cardinal symbol K' which we introduced on p. 167. K' is a symbol satisfying $\sin \pi K' = 0$, and its eigenvalues are the whole set of integers positive and negative. Wave mechanics thus brings the integers (which form the whole material of our ordinary arithmetic) into its purview as the eigenvalues of one of its symbolic operators. Introduced in this way the integers are concepts unassociated with the procedure of counting. Counting, if it is introduced at all, is defined in terms of the eigenvalues of K', i.e. the integers, instead of vice versa. The step which we make from 3 to 4 in counting is a transition—a quantum jump—of a physical characteristic of a system from one eigenvalue to another. The transition of a system from a state of threeness to a state of fourness is only one of many kinds of quantum jump which the system can undergo, and is not differentiated from other quantum jumps in general wave-mechanical theory.

The material, or operand, on which the symbolic operators work is called the wave function of the system. When supplied with certain material, K' reduces to the number 4; we then say that the number of particles in the system represented by the operand is 4; and similarly for other numbers. It should be understood that this is not a special system of interpretation invented for the symbol K'; it is a bringing into line of "number of particles" with the other physical quantities descriptive of the system, which in wave mechanics have each their appropriate symbols reducible to different numbers (not usually integers) according to the wave function supplied to them to operate on. Often the material supplied—the wave function—is such that the operating symbol is not reducible to any number; for that system the physical quantity represented by the symbol has not a definite value, but there are methods of calculating an "expectation value"—a value associated with some degree of uncertainty. This may happen also in the case of the number of particles, if the knowledge represented by the wave function is sufficient only to give a probable estimate of the number.

The fact that K', if it reduces to a number at all, is always an integer discriminates it from most of the other symbolic operators. This condition secures that we never catch ourselves saying that the number of particles in a system is precisely $3\frac{3}{4}$. It is true that there are other operators associated with a physical system which have only integral eigenvalues; but that is because particles are not the only things we can count—or rather for which we can devise a substitute for counting. It will be remembered that "atomicity" extends to radiation (photons) and to angular momentum, as well as to material particles.

In swallowing up arithmetic, quantum theory has a little overreached itself. To comprise the whole of the integers the cardinal operator must satisfy $\sin \pi K' = 0$. But we have noticed that, although this is the equation usually employed, it is only an approximation; and if we use the exact equation the series of integers represented by K' stops at a rather high number which we will call N. There is therefore a distinction between quantum arithmetic and Pythagorean arithmetic. There is no infinity in quantum arithmetic, and the numbers stop at a highest number N. So that the principle by which the number called "the number of particles in a system" is assigned to the system makes it impossible to assign numbers higher than N, which do not occur in quantum arithmetic.

The cosmical number N takes the place of infinity in relativistic quantum arithmetic in much the same way that the velocity of light takes the place of infinite velocity in elementary relativity theory. So far, I have not said anything as to the way in which N is determined; I have been concerned only with the setting in which it appears. But now that we have dragged to light the nature of the device by which number is assigned to the uncountable, I think it will be clear that in claiming to determine *a priori* the number of elementary particles in the universe we are not usurping a prerogative which has usually been ascribed to the Creator of the universe.

A further word may be said as to the uncountability of electrons. It may be objected that we actually do count electrons in a Wilson chamber, where their tracks are made visible by an ingenious device. But how many electrons are there in a Wilson chamber? Something of the order 10^{20}. And how many do we count? A dozen or so. We count up to about twelve and then stop; not because we are tired, but because there is no way of continuing. I do not think that conflicts with my statement that counting, which I take to mean systematic enumeration, is inapplicable to electrons.

In general the only countable particles are those which possess exceptionally high velocities. It is true that by examining these we can derive a ratio of mass to number, which, if assumed to hold also for uncountable particles, enables us to deduce the number from the mass. But I am not denying that the physicists have found a rational and consistent way of extending the definition of number to uncountable systems. The point is that they *have* extended the definition. So that when I, obediently following their definition, speak of the number of particles in the universe, you must not think I mean that there are N discrete entities, put there by the Creator, ready to be enumerated.

II

The theoretical calculation of the cosmical number N depends on the fact that a measurement involves four entities and is therefore associated with a quadruple existence symbol. From this it appears that the cosmical number must be the total number of independent quadruple wave functions, which is found to be $2 \times 136 \times 2^{256}$. This is the number of protons *and* electrons. The number of protons is 136×2^{256}, which is the number given in full at the beginning of this chapter.

The following is, I think, a legitimate way of regarding the construction of this number. The number 136 is characteristic of the group structure of the quadruple existence symbols; and for that reason it also turns up in the theory of the other numerical constants of nature (the fine-structure constant and the mass-ratio). The structure pattern is an interlacing of the relations of 136 elements, which in the present application are identified with 136 condensed states. The cardinal symbol K' associated with each condensed state represents an arithmetic in which the highest integer is 2^{256}. Finally the number is doubled because we start with half the particles (or half the "existence" of the particles) incorporated in the uranoid; so that the negative integers representing subtraction of particles from the uranoid must be taken into account as well as the positive integers representing addition.*

The number $2.136.2^{256}$ is associated with quadruple existence symbols. The corresponding numbers associated with double and simple symbols are $2.10.2^{16}$ and $2.3.2^4$. The latter number is 96. We foresaw (p. 169) that the number 4, associated with measurement, would be incorporated in some form in our world-picture of the results of measurement, though we realised that it might appear rather disguised. We now find that one of its disguises is the raising of the number of particles in the universe from 96 to $3 \cdot 145 . 10^{79}$.

I have told you what I believe to be the true story of the cosmical number N. What should we conclude from it?

To put it crudely, we have *debunked N*. It is not an enumeration of a crowd of discrete particles constituting the objective universe. Since it is merely a number foisted on us by quantum theory, being associated in an *a priori* way with its methods of analysis, is it any longer of interest? I do not think its scientific interest is at all affected. Intrinsically the number of particles in the universe, even if it were genuine, would be a matter of rather trivial curiosity. The number is scientifically important because it keeps cropping up in more prosaic problems. It fixes the ratio of the electrical to the gravitational force between a proton and electron—a quantity which practical physicists have been at great pains to determine. Actually their determinations verify the value we have found to about one part in 500. It also fixes the speed of recession of the distant nebulae which produces "the expansion of the universe". The astronomical data are

---

* From this point of view the "highest integer" in quantum arithmetic is 2^{256}. To form N we then add together 2×136 such numbers by ordinary arithmetic.

rather rough, but they confirm the calculated value of N to within 25 per cent. It also fixes the range of the peculiar forces which govern the equilibrium of the atomic nucleus. The agreement with the experimental value is within 1 per cent.

I have singled out N for attention because, of all the knowledge comprised in fundamental physics, knowledge of the number of elementary particles had seemed least likely to be tainted with subjectivity. It was therefore particularly suitable for a test case. But the same subjectivity appears everywhere, and is usually not so difficult to discern. The whole scheme of physical law is debunked, if you like to put it that way. But debunking the laws of optics will not put out the sun's light; debunking the law of gravitation will not prevent us from falling down stairs; debunking the laws of ballistics will not put a stop to war. Even if the mystery is torn from them, the laws of our semi-subjective universe are valid in that universe, and in the technical discoveries and inventions of science will continue to bear fruit for good or evil.

The big number, given at the beginning of this chapter, has somehow got into the scheme of physics. Who was responsible for putting it there? There are a number of suspects. We naturally examine first those who constructed the method of wave mechanics; but I think they clear themselves. Suspicion rests more heavily on the man who first made electrons—we reject his plea that he only found them. But he too must be acquitted. In the end there seems to be no possible verdict but "Natural Causes". It is just the primitive forms of thought working themselves out, and claiming everyone who takes part in the development of physics as their tool. To the argument that, even if there has been no culpable negligence, there must have been a little carelessness in letting a number like that slip in, we can answer that numbers, once they get into a subject, have a way of breeding, and this number of 80 digits is, as it were, only the grandchild of the number 96.

A slight reddening of the light of distant galaxies was the first clue to the cosmical number. That is the traditional *a posteriori* method of science. But to the observer of observers, the exact value of the cosmical number is implicit in his first glimpse of an experimental physicist:

I lifted up mine eyes again, and looked, and behold a man with a measuring line in his hand.*

III

Eighteen years ago I was responsible for a remark which has often been quoted: †

It is one thing for the human mind to extract from the phenomena of nature the laws which it has itself put into them; it may be a far harder thing to extract laws over which it has had no control. It is even possible that laws which have not their origin in the mind may be irrational, and we can never succeed in formulating them.

This seems to be coming true, though not in the way that then suggested itself. I had in mind the phenomena of quanta and atomic physics, which at that time completely baffled our efforts to formulate a rational system of law. It was already apparent that the principal laws of molar physics were mind-made—the result of the sensory and intellectual equipment through which we derive our observational knowledge—and were not laws of governance of the objective universe. The suggestion was that in quantum theory we for the first time came up against the true laws of governance of the objective universe. If so, the task was presumably much more difficult than merely rediscovering our own frame of thought.

* Zechariah, ii, 1.   † *Space, Time and Gravitation*, p. 200.

Since then microscopic physics has made great progress, and its laws have turned out to be comprehensible to the mind; but, as I have endeavoured to show, it also turns out that they have been imposed by the mind—by our forms of thought—in the same way that the molar laws are imposed. Meanwhile a new situation in regard to laws of objective origin has arisen, because the system of physics is no longer deterministic. The totality of mind-made law does not impose determinism. It is in the undetermined behaviour, for which room is left within the complete scheme of physical law at present recognised, that the governing laws (if any) of the objective universe must appear. Eighteen years have therefore not brought us any nearer to a formulation of the objective laws of governance; the only difference is that what I then described as possibly irrational behaviour is now described as undetermined behaviour.

In current physical theory the undetermined element in the behaviour of a system is treated as a matter of chance. If there were serious deviations from the law of chance, observation and theory would not agree. We may therefore say that it is a hypothesis in physics, supported by observation, that there are no objective laws of governance—unless chance is described as a law.

Nevertheless, if we take a wider view than that of physics, I think it would be misleading to regard chance as the characteristic feature of the objective world. The denial of objective laws of governance is not so much a hypothesis of physics as a limitation of its subject matter. Deviations from chance occur, but they are regarded as manifestations of something outside physics, namely consciousness or (more debatably) life. There is in a human being some portion of the brain, perhaps a mere speck of brain-matter, perhaps an extensive region, in which the physical effects of his volitions begin, and from which they are propagated to the nerves and muscles which translate the volition into action. We will call this portion of the brain-matter "conscious matter". It must be exactly like inorganic matter in its obedience to the fundamental laws of physics which, being of epistemological origin, are compulsory for all matter; but it cannot be identical in all respects with inorganic matter, for that would reduce the body to an automaton acting independently of consciousness. The difference must necessarily lie in the undetermined part of the behaviour; the part of the behaviour which is undetermined by the fundamental laws of physics must in conscious matter be governed by objective law or direction instead of being wholly a field of chance.

The term "law of chance" tends to mislead, because it is applied to what is merely an absence of law in the usual sense of the term. It is clearer to describe the conditions by reference to correlation. The hypothesis of current physical theory, which is confirmed by observation of inorganic phenomena, is that there is no correlation of the undetermined behaviour of the individual particles.

Accordingly the distinction between ordinary matter and conscious matter is that in ordinary matter there is no correlation in the undetermined parts of the behaviours of the particles, whereas in conscious matter correlation may occur. Such correlation is looked upon as an interference with the ordinary course of nature, due to the association of consciousness with the matter; in other words, it is the physical aspect of a volition. This does not mean that, in order to execute a volition, consciousness must direct each individual particle in such a way that correlation occurs. The particles are merely a representation of our knowledge in the frame of thought corresponding to the concept of analysis and the atomic concept. When we apply the system of analysis which gives this representation, we cannot foresee whether the resulting particles will have correlated or uncorrelated behaviour; that depends entirely on the objective characteristics of whatever it is that we are analysing. When non-correlation is assumed, as is customary in physics, it is assumed as a hypothesis. But, without making any hypothesis, we can say that correlation and non-correlation are representations in our frame of thought of different objective characteristics; and since non-correlation admittedly represents the objective characteristic of systems to which the ordinary formulae of physics apply, correlation must represent another objective characteristic which—since it is not characteristic of systems to which the formulae of physics apply—is regarded by us as something "outside physics".

In the discussion of freewill provoked by the modern physical theories, it has, I think, generally been assumed that, since the ordinary laws of inorganic matter leave its behaviour undetermined within a certain narrow range, there can be no scientific objection to allowing a volition of consciousness to decide the exact behaviour within the limits of the aforesaid range. I will call this hypothesis *A*. For any system on a molar scale the permitted range is exceedingly small; and very far-fetched suppositions are necessary to enable volition, working in so small a range, to produce large muscular movements. To obtain a wider range we must admit correlation of the behaviour of the particles. This is the theory we have been discussing, and will be called hypothesis *B*. In former writings I have advocated hypothesis *B* mainly on the ground of the inadequacy of hypothesis *A*; but in the present mode of approach hypothesis *B* presents itself as the obvious and natural solution.

Although leading to the same conclusion, my earlier discussions★ were marred by a failure to recognise that hypothesis *A* is nonsense; so that I was more apologetic than I need have been for going beyond it. There is no half-way house between random and correlated behaviour. Either the behaviour is wholly a matter of chance, in which case

★ *The Nature of the Physical World*, pp. 310–315. *New Pathways in Science*, p. 88.

the precise behaviour within the Heisenberg limits of uncertainty depends on chance and not on volition. Or it is not
wholly a matter of chance, in which case the Heisenberg limits,
which are calculated on the assumption of non-correlation,
are irrelevant. If we apply the law of chance to the tossing
of a coin, the number of heads in 1000 throws is undetermined within the limits, say, 450 to 550. But if a coin-
tossing machine is used which picks up and throws the coin
not entirely at random, the non-chance element is not a
factor deciding which number between 450 and 550 will
turn up; a correlation, or systematic tendency in tossing,
may produce any number of heads from 0 to 1000.

The fallacy of hypothesis A was that it assumed the
behaviour to be restricted by the ordinary laws of physics
including the hypothesis of non-correlation or "law of
chance", and then to be further restricted (or decided) by a
non-chance factor (volition). But we cannot suppose the
behaviour to be restricted by chance and non-chance (non-
correlation and correlation) simultaneously. The applicability
of the law of chance is a hypothesis; the admission that the
behaviour is not governed solely by chance denies the hypothesis. So if we admit volition at all, we must not forget
first to remove the hypothesis of chance if we have been
applying it; in particular we must drop the Heisenberg limits
which apply only to non-correlated behaviour. If volition
operates on the system, it does so without regard to the
Heisenberg limits. Its only limits are those imposed by the
fundamental epistemological laws.

Our volitions are not entirely unconsequential; so that
there must be laws of some kind applying to them and
connecting them with other constituents of consciousness,
though such laws are not expected to be of the mathematically exact type characteristic of subjective law. Primarily the sphere of objective law is the interplay of
thoughts, emotions, memories and volitions in conscious-

ness. In controlling volitions objective law controls also the correlations which are the physical counterparts of volitions.

Our philosophy has led to the view that in so far as we can separate the subjective and objective elements in our experience, the subjective is to be identified with the physical and the objective with the conscious and spiritual aspects of experience. To this we now add, as a helpful analogy provided it is not pressed too far, that conscious purpose is the "matter" and chance the "empty space" of the objective world. In the physical universe matter occupies only a small region compared with the empty space; but, rightly or wrongly, we look on it as the more significant part. In the same way we look on consciousness as the significant part of the objective universe, though it appears to occur only in isolated centres in a background of chaos.

IV

I am about to turn from the scientific to the philosophical setting of scientific epistemology. This is accordingly a suitable place at which to make a comparison with the most commonly accepted view of scientific philosophy. The following statement is fairly typical:

That science is concerned with the rational correlation of experience rather than with the discovery of fragments of absolute truth about an external world is a view which is now widely accepted.*

I think that the average physicist, in so far as he holds any philosophical view at all about his science, would assent. The phrase "rational correlation of experience" has a savour of orthodoxy which makes it a safe gambit for applause. The repudiation of more adventurous aims gives a comfortable feeling of modesty—all the more agreeable if we fancy

* Unsigned review, *Phil. Mag.*, vol. 25, p. 814, 1938.

that someone else is being told off. For my own part I accept the statement, provided that "science" is understood to mean "physics". It has taken me nearly twenty years to accept it; but by steady mastication during that period I have managed to swallow it all down bit by bit. Consequently I am rather flabbergasted by the light-hearted way in which this pronouncement, carrying the most profound implications both for philosophy and for physics, is commonly made and accepted.

I have no serious quarrel with the average physicist over his philosophical creed—except that he forgets all about it in practice. My puzzle is why a belief that physics is concerned with the correlation of experience and not with absolute truth about the external world should usually be accompanied by a steady refusal to treat theoretical physics as a description of correlations of experience and an insistence on treating it as a description of the contents of an absolute objective world. If I am in any way heterodox, it is because it seems to me a consequence of accepting the belief, that we shall get nearer to whatever truth is to be found in physics by seeking and employing conceptions suitable for the expression of correlations of experience instead of conceptions suitable for the description of an absolute world.

The statement evidently means that the methods of physics are incapable of discovering fragments of absolute truth about an external world; for we should have no right to withhold from mankind the absolute truth about the external world if it were within our reach. If the laboratories, built and endowed at great expense, could assist in the discovery of absolute truth about the external world, it would be reprehensible to discourage their use for this purpose. But the assertion that the methods of physics cannot reveal absolute (objective) truth or even fragments of absolute truth, concedes my main point that the knowledge obtained by them is wholly subjective. Indeed it concedes it far too readily;

for the assertion is one that ought only to be made after prolonged investigation. As I have pointed out, sciences other than physics and chemistry are not so limited in their scope. The discovery of unmistakeable signs of intelligent life on another planet would be hailed as an epoch-making astronomical achievement; it can scarcely be denied that it would be the discovery of a fragment of absolute truth about the world external to us.

Keeping to physics, the commonly accepted scientific philosophy is that it is not concerned with the discovery of absolute truth about the external world, and its laws are not fragments of absolute truth about the external world, or, as I have put it, they are not laws of the objective world. What then are they, and how is it that we find them in our correlations of experience? Until we can see, by an examination of the procedure of correlation of our observational experience, how these highly complex laws can have got into it subjectively, it seems premature to accept a philosophy which cuts us off from all other possible explanations of their origin. This is the examination that we have been conducting.

The end of our journey is rather a bathos after so much toil. Instead of struggling up to a lonely peak, we have reached an encampment of believers, who tell us "That is what we have been asserting for years". Presumably they will welcome with open arms the toilworn travellers who have at last found a resting place in the true faith. All the same I am a bit dubious about that welcome. Perhaps the assertion, like many a religious creed, was intended only to be recited and applauded. Anyone who *believes* it is a bit of a heretic.

CHAPTER XII

THE BEGINNINGS OF KNOWLEDGE

I

WE turn now to consider the relation between physical knowledge and human experience as a whole. Two modes of approach are open to us:

(1) We may develop our general philosophy from the beginning, trusting that the experience gained in an intensive study of one branch may assist us to a right decision on some of the questions over which philosophers have been divided.

(2) We may inquire which of the existing systems of philosophy harmonises best with the conclusions reached in scientific epistemology.

The first course brings us into the game as *players*, the second as *umpires*.

If we choose the second course, we (as scientists) naturally take the view that a philosophical system which is in disaccord with the results of scientific epistemology must be rejected. It is more likely that there is an error in the assumptions or logic of the general philosophy than that the epistemological principles, whose consequences have been tested in innumerable practical applications, are unsound. But, leaving aside this claim to adjudicate on ultimate truth, we may well concentrate on a nearer aim. If science is the study of the rational correlation of experience, the endeavour of the scientific philosopher must be to extend this rational correlation from a limited field of experience to the whole of experience. His task is to provide a general philosophy which a scientist can accept *without throwing over his scientific beliefs*. If our scientific enlightenment has not yet reached the stage at which we are ripe to receive pure philosophical truth, it is none the less urgent to integrate our thought into a consistent philosophy which goes as far towards the truth as the present limitations of science permit.

The scientific intruder feels himself under a disadvantage if he follows the first course. Ostensibly he is treating problems which have been the life-study of hundreds better equipped on most points than himself. His one advantage, which justifies the intrusion, is kept in the background, namely that scientific epistemology gives him a foreknowledge of certain of the conclusions to which the argument must lead, or at least of certain conclusions which it must contrive to avoid. Considerations of caution therefore strongly incline me to the second course; but considerations of clearness compel me to adopt the first. There seems no escape from the rule that to make clear a system of thought one must begin at the beginning. Desire for clarity sometimes requires us to make clear things which it would be safer to leave vague; it exposes to attack outposts of our thought which may not be essential to the main position. My purpose in this book is to make certain specific contributions to philosophy rather than to set forth a complete philosophic system; but contributions cannot be left suspended *in vacuo* or (still worse) in an atmosphere hostile to the scientific thought in which they originate, and I therefore feel obliged to sketch in a possible background for them which will, I hope, make their place in general philosophy better understood.

It is, I think, inadvisable to try to describe a scientifically grounded philosophy by the labels of the older philosophical systems. To accept such a label would make the scientist a party to controversies in which he has no interest, even if he does not condemn them as altogether meaningless. But if it were necessary to choose a leader from among the older philosophers, there can be no doubt that our choice would be Kant. We do not accept the Kantian label; but, as a matter of acknowledgment, it is right to say that Kant anticipated to a remarkable extent the ideas to which we are now being impelled by the modern developments of physics.

Reference may also be made to another general philosophical system, namely *logical positivism*. Our insistence that physical quantities are to be defined in such a way that the assertions of physics admit of observational verification, may suggest an affinity with logical positivism. The meaning of a scientific statement is to be ascertained by reference to the steps which would be taken to verify it. This will be recognised as a tenet of logical positivism—only it is there extended to all statements. When it is limited, as here, to items of physical knowledge, it is in no sense a philosophical tenet; it is only a bringing into line of the language of theoretical and of experimental physics, so that we may not claim the support of observation for assertions which have no observational foundation. If it were a general characteristic of knowledge, it would not be so useful to us in discriminating physical knowledge from other kinds of knowledge. We are therefore not particularly predisposed to favour the more general assertion of logical positivism that the meaning of all non-tautological statements is to be ascertained in the same way, namely by reference to the procedure of verifying them.

II

The comparison with logical positivism forms a useful opening to an inquiry into the nature of other types of knowledge. If I say to you "I am very tired", you know what I mean, because you have felt tired yourself. You may attempt verification of the statement by looking out for confirmatory symptoms in my behaviour; but even if the symptoms provided an infallible test, the meaning of the statement is not ascertainable by reference to them. The statement *means*

"I am very tired"; it does not *mean* "I am going to yawn".

It must be admitted that the knowledge conveyed by the statement is limited—much more limited than at first appears. You know what I mean because I appeal to a feeling which you have experienced yourself. But you know only your own feeling of tiredness; you cannot know mine. Your understanding of my meaning (if you do understand it) is a *sympathetic understanding*. Sympathetic knowledge, if we decide to admit it as knowledge, must be distinguished both from direct knowledge, such as we have of our feelings, and structural knowledge, such as we have of the physical universe.

Is it right to count sympathetic understanding as knowledge? So far as physical science is concerned, the answer is unimportant; for we have seen that only a structural knowledge of the sensations in consciousness, whether our own or anyone else's, is used in physics; and this can be freely communicated without appeal to sympathetic understanding of the sensations. But if we are to see physical science in its right relation to other branches of human thought, it is necessary to come to a decision about sympathetic knowledge.

One possibility is to deny altogether the validity of sympathetic understanding, treating it as a way of persuading ourselves that we understand something which we don't. If so, the statement "I am very tired" must be entirely without meaning for you; for it does not mean that I am experiencing *your* feeling of tiredness, nor does it refer to the physical symptoms of my tiredness which would have a meaning for you. Its meaning—for the one person for whom it has a meaning—then seems to fall within the rule of logical positivism, namely that it is to be ascertained by reference to the procedure of verifying it. Suppose that I become uncertain: Is it a feeling of tiredness or a feeling of repletion which is making me disinclined for activity? The verification would, I suppose, consist in calling up from memory an adopted standard feeling of tiredness and comparing my present feeling with the standard. The verification of this knowledge of tiredness is essentially the same as the verification of knowledge of length, except that I alone can perform the verification.

But, before coming to a decision, we should notice that a very similar difficulty arises in regard to *memory* of our own feelings. When I examine the totality of my knowledge, I find that part of it consists of direct awareness of my feelings, but a great deal more consists of memory of my feelings. The memory is something of which I am directly aware; but, as an object of direct awareness, it is quite different from the feeling itself. No one can mistake the memory of a toothache for a toothache.

It is therefore incorrect to say that I have direct awareness of my own sensations, unless the term "sensation" is confined to sensations occurring at the present moment—a limitation contrary to common usage. As regards former sensations, the "I" that is assembling its knowledge has lost the direct awareness that it once had, and knows them only by memory. Thus, leaving aside a transitory knowledge of what I feel at the moment, the stable part of my knowledge is a knowledge of those duller impressions called memories of sensations, or, as it is perhaps clearer to call them, remembered-sensations. I am directly aware of remembered-sensations; but it is a universal form of thought that a remembered-sensation is to be regarded, not as a constituent of knowledge important in itself, but as an indirect apprehension of a past sensation of which I have not direct awareness. It is, in short, a sympathetic knowledge of the past sensation.

The difference between this sympathetic understanding of our own past feelings and sympathetic understanding of other people's feelings is lessened as we go back to distant memories. My memories of feelings go back to those of a small boy who seems much more of a stranger to me now than many of my present acquaintances. I doubt whether I really know what things felt like, tasted like, looked like to him any better than I know what they feel, taste, and look like to a man I have just been talking with.

If we deny all sympathetic knowledge, our outlook becomes not merely solipsistic but ultra-solipsistic. We contemplate a world in which only the momentary self exists; for we deny *all* knowledge of a self preceding it. The earlier self, of which memory tells us, is dismissed as a construct of the supposed sympathetic understanding which persuades us we have a knowledge which we have not. On the other hand, if we admit sympathetic understanding even of the limited kind required for the interpretation of memories, we admit a third kind of knowledge which is neither structural knowledge nor direct awareness. It does not follow that our sympathetic understanding of other persons' feelings must also be admitted to be genuine knowledge; but a leading objection to its possible genuineness is overridden.

Looking at the question broadly, I do not think we can deny a place in the sum of human knowledge to knowledge apprehended only by sympathetic understanding. Since we recognise that there is a subjective element in knowledge, it is necessary to indicate clearly the subject-partner whose knowledge we are considering. The subject-partner in "human knowledge" is not to be identified with the subject-partner in "my knowledge"; his precise specification must depend on our conception of human nature. If we regard the sympathetic faculty as a morbid excrescence, we are doubtless justified in rejecting the knowledge which it pretends to apprehend; as the blind men in Wells's story, who regarded sight as a morbid irritation of the brain due to the diseased condition of two soft depressions in the face, were justified according to their lights in rejecting the visual knowledge of the stranger. But how can I define human nature (as distinct from my particular nature) unless I concede the validity of my supposed understanding of other persons' minds? Without the sympathetic faculty which enables me to recognise myself, not as an individual *mei generis*, but as an element of a social complex, the conception of "human knowledge" could not arise; and it would therefore seem illogical to reject this faculty in defining the extent of human knowledge.

No one believes in solipsism, and very few even assert that they do. Those who are obsessed by the word "existence" come somehow to the conclusion that other consciousnesses besides their own exist; that is to say, other consciousnesses can be the subject of that mysterious sentence which they never finish. Those who adopt the epistemological approach take for their subject matter a knowledge which embodies the experiences of other individuals on the same footing as their own experience. Formally this is non-committal; it is not necessary to assign reasons for choosing a particular theme of study. But undoubtedly the choice is determined by a conviction, akin to religious conviction, that this co-operative knowledge is the most worth while. This conviction is inconsistent with a solipsistic outlook.

It would be meaningless to attribute consciousness to another man without knowing at all what we are attributing to him. But consciousness is not a structural concept describable by purely structural knowledge; nor is the consciousness that we attribute to another man anything of which we have direct awareness, since it is not our own consciousness. It follows that, if our recognition of conscious beings other than ourselves has any meaning at all, their consciousness must be something of which we have a knowledge which is neither structural knowledge nor direct awareness; and any description of it must be expressed in terms of the third kind of knowledge which we have called sympathetic understanding. We commonly define the consciousness of another person as something which has a general kind of likeness to our own consciousness. But we can scarcely couple a general likeness with complete dissimilarity of detail—with the assertion that there is nothing in another man's consciousness that is not completely misrepresented by its supposed counterpart in our own. It seems necessary therefore to couple with sympathetic understanding of another consciousness some measure of sympathetic understanding of the feelings belonging to it.

Our conclusion that sympathetic knowledge must be admitted (as the only alternative to solipsism) does not imply that the knowledge of another person's feelings which we commonly suppose ourselves to possess is to be accepted without question. Experience of colour-blindness teaches us that one man's colour sensations may not be comparable with another's. It seems impossible to attach any meaning to the question whether your sensation of red is like my sensation of red. I hesitate to say that it is equally meaningless to say that your sensation of red is more like my sensation of red than my sensation of a musical note—though I confess I do not see a meaning. When we go beyond sensation and consider similar questions or statements covering, let us say, the following kinds of feeling—the passage of time, a guilty conscience, the taste of sugar, being in love, toothache, amusement at a joke—our reason revolts altogether. A consciousness in which there had been a general post of these feelings could not be admitted to be a consciousness at all.

Happily for the physicist he has a domain independent of sympathetic knowledge, and he can leave to others, better equipped, the task of sorting out the residuum of truth in our common conception of what another man's mind would be like if we could get inside it. We therefore only go far enough to show what are the essentials of a general philosophical outlook which will not place us in the dilemma of either (a) denying that there is any knowledge other than physical knowledge or (b) relapsing into the solipsism which we repudiate at the very beginning of physical science.

III

Let us now consider the common root from which scientific and all other knowledge must arise. The only subject presented to me for study is the content of my consciousness. According to the usual description, this is a heterogeneous collection of sensations, emotions, conceptions, memories, etc. The raw materials of knowledge and the manufactured products of intellectual activity exist side by side in this collection. We wish to pick out the raw material—the primitive data unspoiled by the intervention of habitual forms of thought.

It must, I think, be recognised that this is an unattainable ideal. Our faculty of sensory perception is modified by training; and it is impossible to conceive it divested altogether of the training forced on it by the conditions of life and adaptation to environment. I do not think that sensation, as we know it, could exist without an activity of mind which concentrates, compares and distinguishes. What we call a sensation can never be purely sensory. But that is a question better left to psychologists. In any case the practical difficulty exists. We shall probe down towards the roots of knowledge; but the most primitive data we can reach will not be wholly independent of the primitive forms of thought. We just cannot help being brainy, and must try to make the best of it.

It is indeed one of the primitive forms of thought, namely the concept of analysis, which presents the unity of consciousness to us in the form of a collection of sensations, emotions, etc. The analysis of consciousness into parts presents the same problems as the analysis of the physical universe into parts.

By what criterion is the accepted system of analysis distinguished from other possible systems of analysis? Is the ideal part self-sufficient, so that without contradiction it can be thought of as isolated from the rest?

I shall take the view that consciousness is a whole which we analyse into parts, and not a number of discrete units (sensations, emotions, thoughts, etc.) which are spoken of collectively as a consciousness. Also I take it that our ordinary analysis is rather crude, and that there is overlapping and interaction of the parts. What we call a single sensation is not strictly separable from the environment of emotion, memory, conceptual form, etc., in which it occurs.

At this meeting point of all branches of knowledge, we have to distinguish the branch which leads to knowledge of the physical universe. The raw material for this knowledge is contained in the parts of consciousness called sensations or sensory impressions. The two names have not quite the same significance; "sensation" imputes only those characteristics of which we are directly aware, whereas "sensory impression" refers to a postulated connection with physical stimuli transmitted through the sense organs. At this stage, while we are still seeking a route to the physical universe, and thence to our bodies and sense organs, the term "sensory impression" is premature. There is danger of a vicious circle if we define the physical universe by its general connection with the structure of sensation in consciousness, and then use defined portions of the physical universe (sense organs) to determine what part of our consciousness the name "sensation" refers to. The question therefore arises whether the distinction between sensations and the rest of consciousness is one of which we are directly aware, or whether it is imported later when we have learnt about sensory impressions. I think the answer is that by direct knowledge we can make an initial classification distinguishing sensations from the other contents of consciousness; but this is elaborated into, and ultimately superseded by, a more precise classification which identifies sensations with sersory impressions.

This question is very much simplified by the fact that, although all our senses may be used for exploring the physical universe, most of them are redundant and merely corroborate the information which can be obtained by others. It is therefore unnecessary to know at this stage the exact scope of the term "sensation". It is sufficient if we can distinguish by direct awareness a particular class of sensations, which by itself is sufficient to reveal all that is known of the physical universe. Ideally all our knowledge of the physical universe could have been reached by visual sensation alone—in fact, by the simplest form of visual sensation, colourless and non-stereoscopic.* We can therefore regard an item of physical knowledge as an assertion of what has been or would be perceived visually. The tests of physiology and experimental psychology, used to discriminate sense impressions from other feelings, can accordingly be described in visual terms. In this way we define the scope of sense impression without making use of preliminary attempts to define by direct awareness the full scope of sensation.

The distinction between sensations and other feelings is not so self-evident a classification as we sometimes think. One border-line case is particularly important. Is our feeling of the passage of time a sensation? We cannot devise a direct scientific test which would be any more conclusive than our introspective judgment is. But general scientific considerations favour the view that our feeling of the going on of time is a sensory impression; that is to say, it is as closely connected with stimuli from the physical world as the sensation of light is. Just as certain physical disturbances entering the brain cells *via* the optic nerves occasion the sensation of light, so a change of entropy, either in the brain cells generally or in special cells, occasions the sensation of

* *New Pathways in Science*, p. 13.

time succession, the moment of greater entropy being *felt* to be the later. I have treated this problem rather fully in earlier writings and need not add more here.*

Alongside the sensations of which I am directly aware, I admit also two kinds of sensation of which I am not directly aware, (1) the sensations which I remember to have had in the past, and (2) the sensations which other people tell me they have or have had. It is an axiom of physical science that, as raw material for knowledge, these are all on the same footing.

The recognition that certain memories are to be treated as a knowledge of past sensations is essential for physical science; because, as we shall see later, the first step towards structural knowledge is a comparison of sensations in one consciousness. The datum of physical science is not awareness of a sensation, but awareness that a sensation is like, or different from, a sensation which we formerly had. Granting this, the sensations of one person alone provide sufficient material for structural analysis; and it would be possible to develop from it a scientific theory which, except that it is presented in an egocentric frame of thought, would agree with ordinary physical theory. But since the analysis would never take us outside a single consciousness, it would give no indication of a world external to that consciousness. The externality of the physical world results from the fact that it is made up of structures found in different consciousnesses.

Thus the recognition of sensations other than our own, though not required until a rather later stage of the discussion, is essential to the derivation of an *external* physical universe. Our direct awareness of certain aural and visual sensations (words heard and read) is postulated to be an indirect knowledge of quite different sensations (described by the words heard and read) occurring elsewhere than in our own

* *The Nature of the Physical World*, p. 100.

consciousness. Solipsism would deny this; and it is by accepting this postulate that physics declares itself anti-solipsistic.

IV

In many languages two verbs are required to cover the meanings of the English verb "know". When we say that we know our own feelings, the meaning usually is *kennen* (connaître), whereas we have in this book been mainly concerned with "know" in the sense of *wissen* (savoir). It is necessary to examine rather carefully the nature of our direct awareness in order to make it clear that it provides data of knowledge in the sense of *Wissenschaft*.

To the question "What are we most directly aware of?" the common answer would be "Feelings, and other parts of the content of consciousness". But this is an idiom of speech. The feeling is itself an awareness. What we may call *sentient awareness* has no grammatical object except itself. My consciousness is my awareness, and the parts of my consciousness—feelings, emotions, etc.—are parts of my awareness; and it is a mere oddity of language which leads us to reiterate the awareness in such phrases as "awareness of feeling". Our purpose now is to show that awareness is sapient as well as sentient; and *sapient awareness* has a grammatical object, namely an item of knowledge.

Consider the statement "I am aware that I feel pain". This means that I know that I feel pain in the same sense that I know any other fact, e.g. that the sun has risen. "Aware" is used here only to distinguish the way I have obtained the knowledge. (My knowledge that the sun has risen is not at all a matter of direct awareness—since it happens to have been foggy all day.) But it is necessary to notice that what I am directly aware of is a certain fact, not that the form of words "I feel pain" is a correct description of the fact. The intervention of a form of words creates an awkward difficulty in discussing the elements of knowledge; the more accurate the description, the more extensively does it draw on our general knowledge, and so distract attention from the particular element of knowledge on which we want to focus discussion. An inexact description is not an ideal refuge from this dilemma; so let us try another way.

Suppose that I suddenly say "Ouch". That will convey to you exactly what was meant to be conveyed by the former statement "I feel pain". It has the great advantage that it does not hint at any psychological theory of what has happened; it does not drag in knowledge not wholly derived from direct awareness, as any attempt at precise description would do. Normally it is an involuntary remark; but it is a pity not to use deliberately an expression which conveys exactly what we mean to convey and no more. A typical element of knowledge acquired by direct awareness is that which we convey to another person by the ejaculation "ouch".

Undoubtedly an item of knowledge is conveyed. When the dentist, in the course of his explorations, asks "Does it hurt?" and I answer "Ouch", he obtains definite information. It is clear that I myself had that information before the dentist; and indeed it was an item of knowledge which I particularly wished to convey to him. It is also clear that the knowledge came to me by direct awareness.

This, I think, leaves no doubt that awareness is not only sentient, but is a means of acquiring items of knowledge (*Wissenschaft*). A confusion arises when such knowledge is put into words, because the choice of exact wording depends on general knowledge which is not as a rule acquired by direct awareness. It is only exceptionally that we can give verbal expression to the knowledge acquired by direct awareness without adulterating it. Usually the verbal expression must be regarded as a pointer—pointing out the knowledge, but not forming part of it.

CHAPTER XIII

THE SYNTHESIS OF KNOWLEDGE

I

In considering the primitive data of knowledge furnished by direct awareness, it is necessary to bear in mind that the description of the datum is not part of the datum. In order that you may know what datum I am referring to, I have to use a form of words as a pointer; but even if (as may occasionally happen) the form of words is an accurate expression of a truth about the datum, it is a truth reached by subsequent investigation and not given to us as a primitive datum.

A stranger in a land, where his resources of language fail him, will open communication by pointing. In this discussion of the origins of knowledge we are in a like position and have to do a good deal of pointing. But as pointing in a literal sense is impossible, we have to point with words and phrases. This use of language for pointing must be distinguished from its use for explicit description which cannot begin until a later stage. Logical inference is not applicable to it, for inferences can only be made from data; and a pointer is not a datum. We do not reject logical thought, but we insist that it shall be applied to the real data.

Thus, in the fundamental problems which come at the beginning of philosophy the form of words is, in general, the last thing to which one should pay attention. Either the wording represents the philosophical views of the prehistoric inventors of language; or it prematurely assumes a truth which it is our business to find out by investigation. Considering again the statement "I am aware that I feel pain", you know what it means because at times you yourself have such an awareness. It serves its function as a pointer; and, if you are satisfied that the speaker is not lying, you can accept it (with the meaning that you have recognised) as a datum of knowledge. But presumably you do not accept as a datum of knowledge the philosophy embodied in the form of the statement—that there is a sentient "I" who feels, and a sapient "I" aware that the sentient "I" feels, with perhaps an infinite regression of "I's" each aware that the one next in order is aware of something. Even if you happen to agree with that philosophy, you realise that it has nothing to do with the knowledge that was being communicated in the statement. A man can be aware of pain without being a philosopher.

Let us consider why the description (though not the datum) introduces two "I's", which we find it difficult to identify completely. It is a consequence of the non-solipsistic outlook that the knower does not usually coincide with the feeler. Other people's sensations are as important as our own; and the usual form of knowledge would be "I know that so-and-so feels pain". When the exceptional case occurs, the form must not be altered; for it would be a solipsism to give our own sensations any kind of priority or distinctiveness in knowledge. Thus the description must indicate the possessor of the knowledge and the possessor of the feeling separately, even when both the knowledge and the feeling are parts of the same consciousness—parts which to a considerable extent overlap. Any attempt to argue from the wording that the two possessors cannot be completely identical is ruled out because it mistakes the function of the form of words which is to *point*. What is pointed at, i.e. the datum, is that the knowing and the feeling are parts of one consciousness distinguished from other consciousnesses by the verbal-pointer "I".

It may be noticed that "I know that" is an *idempotent* phrase (p. 162):

I know that I know that = I know that.

Iteration makes no difference to its pointer-value. That the two phrases mean (i.e. point to) precisely the same thing is seen when we examine the apparent alternative "I do not know that I know that", which is clearly nonsense.* If we represent "A knows that" by the symbol J_A, the statement $J_A J_B$ is normally irreducible; but in the special case $A = B$, we have $J_A J_A = J_A$. The iteration can be repeated any number of times; thus $J_A J_A J_A \ldots J_A = J_A$.

In our ordinary language a feeling is associated with a knowledge, namely a knowledge that the feeling exists. There is no ambiguity in completing this "unfinished sentence"; the feeling exists in, or is part of, a consciousness. For a solipsist this is a truism, since feeling is the name given to a part of consciousness; and there is only one consciousness—his own—for it to be part of. But when we admit more than one consciousness, we make the knowledge more comprehensive than the feeling by adding a pointer indicating the particular consciousness in which the feeling exists or of which it is a part.

II

Since knowledge of the physical world is derived from sensations, let us take for discussion a particular sensation, for example, the sensation described as I-perceive-the-sound-of-the-Greenwich-time-signal. Evidently the description contains information which is no part of the sensation, and is not itself a matter of direct apprehension. We must now ask, Is *any* part of the description a matter of direct apprehension? In particular, have we a direct awareness that the sensation is a subject-object relation, as the form of description implies? I do not think we have. We can, if we like, experiment with the hypothesis that a sensation is, or can be represented as, a relation (perceiving) between a

* It is to be remembered that "know" does not mean "know with certainty" (p. 1).

subject ("I") and an object (a "sensum"); but that is very different from asserting that we are directly aware that it is such a relation. That the experiment is unsuccessful is, I think, shown by the barrenness of realist philosophy. The object-end of the relation is a cul-de-sac. But let us examine more closely the subject-end of the relation.

Hitherto the term "I" has been for us a pointer-word, used to point to a particular consciousness of which the sensation forms part. Equivalently it is a label attached to the consciousness to save the trouble of pointing every time we mention it. When by the concept of analysis we separate the consciousness into a number of sensations, emotions, etc., we attach to each part the label "I"—or, in deference to the grammarians, "my". The modified label does not denote possession except in the sense in which a whole "possesses" parts; it does not postulate an owner distinct from the con-sciousness, who owns all the parts and therefore the whole consciousness. Nevertheless the function of "I" as a label does not exhaust the significance commonly attached to "I". Among the contents of my consciousness is a self-conscious-ness. In the language of subject-object relations we say "I am aware of 'I'". Without endorsing this description of self-consciousness as a subject-object relation, we recognise it as a pointer and admit the primitive datum to which it points. The question then is, What additional significance is given to "I" in connection with this datum of self-consciousness?

We must remember that the concept of analysis is a form of thought; and although its application to consciousness serves certain useful purposes, there is no guarantee that a simple putting together of the analytical parts without binding material will reproduce the whole. Even in the physical universe, where the analysis is applied more system-atically, and greater precautions have been taken to secure non-overlapping and permanent self-sufficiency of the parts, the elementary parts are not strictly separable. Still less is a single sensation strictly separable from the environment of emotion, memory and intellectual activity in which it occurs; nor is it strictly separable from the volition which directs attention to it and the thought which embodies sapient knowledge of it. Thus the consciousness to which a particular sensation belongs concerns it, not only as a label, but as an environment.

I have knowledge of a certain sensation, and I have the further knowledge that it is or was *my* sensation. If I am a non-solipsist, the second statement combines two data. One datum refers to the classification of sensations as belonging to a number of different consciousnesses, and disappears if all the sensations of which I admit having knowledge are in one consciousness. But the other datum is concerned with a positive aspect of "my", not arrived at by contrast with "his", and remains valid even for a solipsist. It is that the sensation is not a self-sufficient element of awareness independent of other elements of awareness, but is one of the parts into which by a somewhat crude dissection we have divided an awareness which is presented to us as a whole. The "I" which is the supposed object of self-consciousness is the correlative of "my" in this second aspect—the *uniting* "my"—in the same way that the "I" which is the supposed subject of verbs of awareness is the correlative of "my" as a label—the *contrasting* "my". The nominative, objective and possessive cases are to be disregarded, since the rules of syntax have not been designed for pointer language. The data pointed at are respectively a contrast with sensations belonging to another consciousness, and a unity of conscious awareness which prevents it from being fully represented as an aggregation of self-sufficient parts.

We may, I think, identify self-consciousness with awareness of this unity of consciousness. In one sense self-consciousness can be counted as a "part" of consciousness, just as the interaction between elementary particles can be counted as a part of the physical universe. But it is not homogeneous with the other parts; and in the stricter sense, in which the meaning of a "part" cannot be dissociated from the system of analysis of which it is a product, self-consciousness is not an analytical part but a residuum which has eluded the analysis.

In the subject-object description of self-consciousness "I am aware of 'I'", the second "I" stands for the unity of consciousness. Distinguishing it as I_2, I_2 is what is left if you imagine me without any of the feelings, thoughts, etc., inventoried by the concept of analysis. These inventoried contents can be varied without modifying the essential "I" associated with them. It may perhaps be objected that this description of I_2 precisely fits the "I" who was fast asleep a few hours ago—which seems to lead to the *reductio ad absurdum* that it is in sleep that the essential "I" emerges from the swarm of thoughts and emotions that ordinarily obscure it. But that is like arguing that the essential qualities of glue are best displayed when it does not contaminate itself by sticking anything. To obtain the I_2, of which we are aware in self-consciousness, thoughts and feelings must be abstracted, not eliminated. The unity of consciousness is manifested *because* there are parts for it to unite.

To sum up: "I" is first a label or pointer-word attached to a particular consciousness, and consequentially to the sensations, emotions, etc. into which the consciousness is divided by the concept of analysis; and secondly, as associated with self-consciousness, it is part of a verbal form "I am aware of 'I'" used to point to a residuum of awareness which eludes the concept of analysis. The phrase points to the datum (of which we have immediate knowledge) that our whole awareness is not fully represented by the parts into which we customarily divide it; in other words, it is a unity and not an assemblage of parts. It appears to be no more than linguistic custom that "I" is made in the first case the subject and in the second case the object of the verb "to be aware".

When we try to get behind the wording, we find nothing to support the view that awareness is a subject-object relation or even a subject-intransitive relation.

III

Let us now turn to the supposed object-end of the relation. For the purposes of physics the only value of the direct awareness described as I-perceive-the-sound-of-the-Greenwich-time-signal is that it can be compared with and in some cases recognised to be the same as another direct awareness which I remember to have had. The typical datum for physics is therefore I-have-a-sensation-which-I-have-had-on-a-former-occasion. Provided that a means can be found of describing the former occasion in a way which will enable other persons to identify it in their own experience (without which the information would be of no value), the datum represents communicable knowledge. It is unnecessary to assume that the person to whom the knowledge is communicated has any sympathetic understanding of my aural sensations; he may be a stone-deaf man unable to imagine what a sense of sound would be like.

The theory of structure described in Chapter IX indicates the way in which this communicable type of knowledge is elaborated and made entirely independent of the non-communicable individual sensations. The "former occasion" is identified by its association with other sensations or groups of sensations in the same consciousness, which in turn are compared with and found to be the same as earlier or later sensations. Finally, out of these comparisons we extract a pattern of interlocking, which can be described mathematically and represents structural knowledge of the sensory content of the consciousness studied.

In the case of visual sensations, the structure is more self-evident. Without referring to memory of former sensations we can detect a pattern in what we see at any moment. It is mainly through visual sensation that our ordinary conception of the physical world is formed. But just because it lends itself so easily to structural investigation, it has been mulled over by our early inexpert gropings; and it is not so easy to make a clean start in separating the mathematical essence of the structure from the form of awareness in which it is contained. Our habit of visualising structure makes it more difficult for us to realise the essential abstractness of structure.

As a result of communicating structural knowledge we soon find that the structural contents of different consciousnesses are not wholly independent. The problem then arises, How are we to represent this interdependence? We may begin with the simple case in which the same structure is found in nearly all consciousnesses with which we can communicate, for example, the structure of the visual sensation which arises when we look at a constellation in the starry heavens. We reject the idea that the occurrence of this highly specialised structure in so many consciousnesses is a coincidence, and thereby commit ourselves to the hypothesis that the many similar structures are reproductions of one original structure. This is the germ of the idea of causation. In the language of causation we attribute the similar structures in the different consciousnesses to a common cause containing the same structure.

A possible hypothesis is that this is an effect of heredity. Normal consciousnesses might contain this particular structure for the same reason that normal bodies contain another particular structure called a liver. This hypothesis, however, is refuted by the occurrence of novae (new stars). These are changes of the structure of the visual sensation, occurring simultaneously in all consciousnesses, for which our common ancestor evidently cannot be held responsible. The common cause cannot be located in any one of the consciousnesses without solipsism, nor can it be located in an ancestral consciousness; therefore it must be located outside any of the recognised forms of consciousness. This realm outside individual consciousness, where the common causes of the sensory structures in different consciousnesses are located, is called "the external world".

By recognising other consciousnesses as coequal with our own we had already committed ourselves to the acceptance of a realm outside the individual consciousness. Nevertheless it is a new step of great magnitude when, by the discovery of similar structures common to all normal consciousnesses, we introduce an external world containing the original structure of which they are the reproductions. Since the external world is introduced as a receptacle of structure, our knowledge of it is limited to structural knowledge; and physical science is the study of this structural knowledge. But, should occasion arise, the function of the external world can be enlarged so as to comprise more than our physical knowledge. If we find reason to be dissatisfied with a purely physical world external to ourselves, there is room for a spiritual interpretation of the "something" of which the physical universe is only the abstract structure.

We do not, to begin with, put forward any theory as to *how* the original structure in the external world comes to be reproduced as a structure of sensations in consciousness; we merely recognise that, ruling out coincidence, the occurrence of the same structure in many consciousnesses is a sign that an original structure exists in a realm outside those consciousnesses. Thus the scene of the grand synthesis is transferred to an external realm, where the scraps of structure which are the originals of the sensation-structures in our own and other consciousnesses, stand like pieces of a jig-saw puzzle waiting to be fitted together. This extremely intricate synthesis is a task which physical science has been slowly accomplishing throughout the ages. Mistakes have often been made. In particular, the earlier theories attempted to weave into the synthesis knowledge which is not purely structural; and it is only in recent years that physical theory has become in form, as well as in fact, a theory of mathematical group-structure. But quite early in the synthesis it was possible to discern some of the steps by which structures in the external world are transferred from their original location to consciousness. That is to say, by fitting together the pieces of structure we obtain a comprehensive structure, which contains not only the original pieces but a mechanism for propagating structure.

In the progress of this synthesis we have learned to set aside the crude instinctive view that "seeing" is a sort of stabbing operation which collects information as a park-keeper collects litter. The structure of our visual sensation of a constellation is reproduced many times over in the external world—in a set of material objects, in light waves, on the retina, in optic nerves, in brain-cells. The reproduction in actual sensation follows at the end of this sequence. When our physical knowledge has reached this stage we are entitled to substitute the term "sensory impression" for sensation. Besides our direct awareness of the sensation, we now have indirect knowledge that it is associated with the nerves and sense organs introduced in the synthesis of structural knowledge. This "theory of sensation" has, of course, been freely used in the development of physical science. It could have been introduced at any stage as a reasonable hypothesis to be tested by experiment. But it is not the logical starting point of an exploration of the foundations of science; and in an examination of the nature of the knowledge comprised in physical science, we must go back farther to a datum independent of theories of sensation, namely that the same structures of sensation occur in more than one consciousness much more frequently than can be explained by coincidence.

IV

As a contrast to the method of physical science, let us see how realist philosophy attempts to treat the object-end of the relation. It seems to me to provide an illustration of the disastrous influence which the verbal forms, imposed on us by the unphilosophical shapers of language, are liable to have on our thought.

The following is a typical introduction to realist philosophy:

> It is clear that whenever I have any kind of experience, whether I am dreaming, thinking, having hallucinations, or merely perceiving, something is dreamt, thought, hallucinated, or perceived, and that my mind has *some* relation to this something.*

The argument goes on to point out that this "something" can have different relations to the mind; for that which is perceived can also be remembered or imagined. It is argued that what is in the mind could not have this variety of relationship to the mind; the "something" is therefore not part of the mind. The conclusion is:

> It is a characteristic at once common and peculiar to all mental acts that they should be aware of something other than themselves. To say of an act that it is mental is, indeed, to say of it that it is an awareness of something other than itself. This conclusion entails the corollary that the "something other" of which there is awareness, is unaffected by the mind's awareness of it. As experienced, in other words, it is precisely what it would be, if it were not being experienced.†

This would be a praiseworthy detective effort if our object were to discover the philosophical views of the pioneers of speech—those originally responsible for the way in which we string words into phrases and sentences. But why this

---

* C. E. M. Joad, *Guide to Philosophy*, p. 66. Joad is not necessarily stating his own view.   † *Ibid*, p. 74.

should be resurrected to serve as a basis of twentieth-century philosophy passes my comprehension.

There is no difference of meaning between "dreaming" and "dreaming a dream", or between "thinking" and "thinking a thought". At first sight "dreaming a dream" seems a purposeless reiteration. But if it is desired to enter into particulars, language provides no way of attaching them to a verb; I am not allowed to say that I was falling-over-a-precipicely-dreaming. I have to give the verb an object, even if it is only a dummy object, and attach to the object the particulars which I wish to add. I therefore state as a description of my dream particulars which might equally well have been given as particulars of my dreaming, if the forms of language had allowed. The realist triumphantly produces this dummy object, and says "You admit then that *something* is dreamt, namely the dream which you have so vividly described". I admit nothing of the kind. All I admit is that the rules of language compel me to talk as if I admitted it.

Similarly "living a life" is the same as "living". Grammatically a life is something that is lived; but in actual meaning my life and my living are the same. It is a tyranny of language which decrees that circumstantial details of a man's life can be given, but not of his living which is considered to be an unanalysable activity. It will be seen that there is great opportunity for a dialectic philosophy, under pretence of clearing up a confusion to introduce one. Thus it is pointed out that "sensation" can either mean "sensing" or that which is "sensed"; and it is suggested that the two meanings have been confused in certain philosophies. But there are not two meanings to be confused—only two grammatical forms with the same meaning. And it is the critics who confuse themselves by introducing a sensum, i.e. something sensed which is distinct from the sensing, in order to provide a second meaning.

The view that activity (expressed by verbs and gerunds) is of a few simple kinds and that variety resides in passivity (expressed by nouns) has purely linguistic origin. The paucity of verb forms is familiar to mathematicians as a difficulty of ordinary speech easily surmounted in their own symbolic language. Thus it is possible to speak of duplicating, triplicating, sesquiduplicating, etc., but this mode of expressing variety of operations is soon abandoned; we use instead one verb-form "multiplying" and transfer all the variety to noun-forms called numbers. Then perhaps it will be said "It is clear that whenever anything is multiplied it must be multiplied by *something*, and this something, e.g. two, is not itself a multiplying but an independent entity, exactly the same when it is a multiplier as when it is not a multiplier". The argument would not have arisen if we had stuck to the terms duplicating, triplicating, etc.; for one does not duplicate *by* anything.

The lack of verb-forms and of phrases for qualifying verb-forms makes it difficult to describe consciousness as what we know it to be—an extremely varied activity. In customary language the variety of our intellectual activity is only to be described as a variety of thoughts not as a variety of our thinking. This makes no difference to the physicist, who is concerned only with structure, since the structure of the thinking is also the structure of the thoughts. But it leads many philosophers to place all the variety in sensa outside consciousness, and restrict consciousness to a few unanalysable activities—perceiving, conceiving, remembering, emoting the variety outside itself. But it is not an essential characteristic of activity that it shall be incapable of sub-classification. Gesticulating, for example, is an activity of many varieties—shrugging the shoulders, waving the arms, shaking the head, etc. We can describe the variety directly, without expanding "gesticulating" into "gesticulating a gesture", and proceeding to classify the gestures. And, so I suppose, realists will not insist that whenever we gesticulate something must be gesticulated, and that the something is unaffected by our gesticulation of it, being indeed precisely what it would be if it were not being gesticulated. Yet I sometimes wonder how a realist would regard the gesture known as "cocking a snook". It would seem clear that something must be cocked; and I fear the only logical conclusion is that there is a realm of existence containing uncocked snooks which are exactly what they would be if they were being cocked—but perhaps that is too dangerous a thought to pursue when philosophers are trying to express what they think of one another!

In the introduction to realism that I have quoted (p. 211), the conception of a sensum distinct from the sensing appears to have a purely linguistic origin; but the important conclusion that the sensum is something external to consciousness is based on the existence of a number of different ways in which it can be related to consciousness. Admitting, for the sake of argument, an object of perception, say a patch of blue colour, which is not the perception itself, I think the number of ways in which it can be mentally apprehended has been exaggerated. There are just two ways; it can be perceived, or it can be imagined. Surveying the content of my consciousness, I may find a perceiving of blue colour or an imagining of blue colour. The difference is unmistakeable, and is intrinsic in the perception or imagining; but the hypothesis of the realists is that it is the same object or sensum that is being apprehended in two different ways. I have only these two kinds of awareness of blue colour; but in the content of my consciousness I may find also thoughts about blue colour which are not an awareness of it, though they may accompany a perception or imagining of it. When the thoughts (intellectual knowledge) and the awareness are lumped together, other varieties of classification are introduced. By intellectual knowledge hallucinations are distinguished from perceptions, though intrinsically they are identical. Similarly rememberings are distinguished from casual imaginings.

As a clue to the relation between perceiving and imagining it is noteworthy that (normally at least) a new elementary sensation cannot be imagined until it has first been perceived. We can invent in imagination new combinations of sensations, but we cannot invent entirely new tastes, colours, pains, etc. It would seem that the first time we perceive a new taste, our consciousness becomes modified in such a way that thereafter an imagining of the taste is possible. We ordinarily say that a memory of the taste is stored up in it. I do not see how this can be reconciled with the realist view that imagining and perceiving are independent relations of consciousness to a sensum outside consciousness.

In the passage that I have quoted it is recognised that, if perceiving is purely a relation between the mind and an external object, the object is not modified by our perceiving of it. It is not clear whether it is also recognised that the mind is not modified. If the mind is modified by the act of perceiving, it is incorrect to describe perceiving as a "relation"; and the argument based on the existence of more than one kind of relation falls to the ground. On the other hand, if neither the mind nor the sensum is modified by the act of perceiving, how is it that it is not until after the perception that a new kind of relation of the mind to the sensum becomes possible, namely remembering or imagining?

V

The occurrence of identical, or closely related, structures of sensation in different consciousnesses provides the logical starting-point of physical science. This develops naturally into a general investigation of the correlations of sensory experience; but by the time we reach this wider problem the main line of treatment has already been settled. The correspondences of structure point to a common cause external to the individual consciousnesses. The correlating medium is therefore conceived as an external world, in which influences emanating from various foci are propagated to the points at which the different consciousnesses are located. In elaborating this conception we have to consider the propagation of influences from one part to another of the external world, not only as a means of conveying messages to consciousness, but as continually redistributing the characteristics of the world, and thereby bringing its various parts into causal connection in time and space. Thus we pass on to the main task of physics, which is to formulate a system of description of the external world and a system of laws applicable to the entities mentioned in the description, which shall be in every respect accordant with the actual correlations of sensory experience. By "accordant with sensory experience" we mean that those portions of its structure which are elements of a sensation structure in a consciousness have a uniform correspondence with the sensations actually experienced in that consciousness.

I have emphasised two features of the knowledge of the external world reached in this way: (a) it is partly subjective, and (b) it is structural knowledge. To some extent these are alternatives; that is to say, if we exhibit physical knowledge in the purely structural form provided by the Theory of Groups, we eliminate a large part of the subjective element which appears in the more commonplace formulations. I do not regard even the group-structure as wholly objective; it is contingent on the deep-rooted forms of thought examined in Chapters VIII, IX and X. But the so-called fundamental laws and constants of physics are not features that can be pointed out in the ultimate group-structure; they are introduced by adapting the knowledge to a form of thought less remote from our familiar outlook. As has been pointed out (p. 117), the frame of thought which corresponds to the outposts of scientific advance is not that in which we assess the results of the advance.

It would be illogical to attribute the similarity of the structures in different consciousnesses to a common cause without allowing to the common cause a status fully as objective as the structures themselves. I therefore take it as axiomatic that the external world must have objective content. But according to our conclusions, the laws of physics are a property of the frame of thought in which we represent our knowledge of the objective content, and thus far physics has been unable to discover any laws applying to the objective content itself. This raises the question, How is it that we are able to make successful predictions of phenomena without knowing any law controlling the objective content of the universe and therefore without knowing how the objective content is going to behave?

Although it is rather the fashion for scientific writers to say that physics is not concerned with objective truth, it would be unsafe to take them at their word. Apparently the statement is intended to closure discussion, rather than to assert a principle whose far-reaching implications invite investigation. Our own conclusion is less sweepingly expressed; but it is meant seriously, and we must examine the difficulties to which it seems to lead.

Much of the difficulty disappears if we keep in mind that *pure* subjectivity is confined to the laws—the regularities—of the physical world. The variety of appearances around us is primarily an objective variety. That a subjective distortion is introduced in our apprehension of things is no more than physicists have been accustomed to admit. We have tried to carry farther than hitherto the sorting of the objective and subjective elements—with perhaps surprising results. But we admit an objective element in the special facts which constitute a large part of our knowledge of the universe around us.

Some conclusions which are of the nature of "special facts" have nevertheless a rather wide generality. It is a special fact that most of space is nearly empty, the matter being aggregated in relatively small islands. No one has suggested that this should be ranked as a fundamental law of physics; we are indeed disposed to think that it is a lately developed feature, the primordial distribution of the matter having been a continuous nebula. Yet for some purposes the normal emptiness of space has much the same importance as a law of physics. In astronomy we often eke out our very limited observational knowledge of the distribution of matter by assuming it as a hypothesis—a casual, not a fundamental, hypothesis.

The recognition of objectivity in the special facts, although allaying one kind of difficulty, makes still more pertinent the question how we are able to make predictions without knowing any law controlling the objective content of the universe. It is not as though we could dismiss the objective content from consideration; for the predictions are predictions of special facts which involve the objective content.

The fact is that by the fundamental epistemological laws alone it is not possible to make any sharp predictions. In actual predictions they are coupled with the law of chance. We have seen (Chapter VI) that the modern system of physics admits only predictions of probability. In deducing a probable result, the uncertainty is narrowed down to the Heisenberg limits by assuming that the undetermined part of the behaviour of the individual particles concerned is uncorrelated. This principle of non-correlation is essential in all predictions definite enough to be the subject of observational test.

We have reached the conclusion (p. 181) that the non-correlation of individual behaviour, in spite of its rather wide generality, is a special fact. It is a special fact that matter is normally unassociated with consciousness, just· as it is a special fact that space is normally empty or nearly empty.

Physics would not have taken the form it has taken if it were the rule, rather than the exception, for matter to be under the influence of conscious volition; but equally physics would not have taken the form it has taken if the matter encountered in normal experience had been distributed continuously as it is in the interior of a star.

It is often pointed out that the primary difference of outlook between the scientist and the savage is that the savage attributes all that he finds mysterious in nature to the activity of demons or other spirits. For the savage any physical object may be possessed of demonic volition, and it is impossible to count on its behaviour except in so far as the directing demon may be amenable to prayer and propitiation. Physical science has made a place for itself by greatly limiting the sphere of demonic activity, so that there is an extensive realm of experience in which behaviour can be counted on and scientific prediction is possible. Great as may be the practical effects of this change, it is a matter of detail (special fact) rather than of principle. Demonic activity (volition) remains, though it is limited to certain centres in men and the higher animals. Prayer and propitiation may still influence the course of physical phenomena when directed to these centres. We now think it ludicrous to imagine that rocks, sea and sky are animated by volitions such as we are aware of in ourselves. It would be thought even more ludicrous to imagine that the volitionless behaviour of rocks, sea and sky extends also to ourselves, were it not that we have scarcely yet recovered from the repressions of 250 years of deterministic physics.

Accordingly we do not regard the principle of non-correlation as one of the fundamental laws of physics. Non-correlation usually applies; but correlation occurs exceptionally, and the result is an unexpectedness of behaviour which is recognised by us as a physical manifestation of conscious volition. In saying that the behaviour is unexpected, we mean unexpected from the point of view of physics, which supplies the gap left by our ignorance of the springs of objective behaviour by assuming non-correlation. Actually the volitional behaviour may be fully expected— it may be an answer to our own request—but this expectation takes into account knowledge of the objective world not comprised in physical science and not reducible to the accepted pattern of physical law. In so far as the comparative rarity of correlation can be considered a law, it is a law of distribution of consciousness rather than a law of the physical world.

In my earlier references to the system of fundamental laws of physics, I should not have ventured peremptorily to exclude the law of chance if current opinion were disposed to include it. But I think the majority would be against including it, although their reason is different from my own. The common view is that where we have a great number of individual systems it is improbable that there will be any correlation of their behaviour unless there is some specific cause producing correlation. But a specific cause of correlation would be described in physics as an interaction, and as such it should be provided for in the ordinary system of laws. On this view the law of chance is purely negative— asserting that there are no further correlations than those provided for in the system of laws already formulated. In short, the law of chance or non-correlation is not one of the fundamental laws of physics but the word "Finis" added when the list is complete.

This argument is based on the synthetic view of world-structure, which starts with individual particles and combines them to form the objects perceptible to our gross senses. Although no really rigorous proof has been found, it seems a reasonable conclusion that such a mode of construction is sufficient to ensure non-correlation; and there is therefore no need to include the principle of non-correlation as an additional hypothesis. But non-correlation appears in a different light according to the analytic view of world-structure, which starts with the gross objects and analyses them into the structural elements which we call individual particles. According to the characteristics of the object analysed we may obtain structural elements with correlated or non-correlated behaviour. When we find non-correlation, the independence is not an individual possession of each particle; it is characteristic only of the particular combination that is studied. The analytic view therefore does not automatically impose the principle of non-correlation. This is unlike the synthetic view in which independence—indifference to what other particles are doing—is assumed to be an unconditional characteristic of each particle, so that correlated behaviour of the particles in an aggregated system would be contrary to nature.

We accept the analytic view which provides no *a priori* reason for non-correlation. But, as already explained, we do not admit a general principle or law of non-correlation. Instead we admit a principle of *rarity* of correlation as a special fact about the world in its present condition.

VI

Throughout this discussion we have adhered to the epistemological mode of approach. For us *knowledge* has been the one thing that counts. The spiritual element in man appears in our survey as something which *knows*—something to be looted for the treasure of knowledge it contains. With the ruthlessness of a collector we carry off the treasure to our museum, there to be systematically arranged and displayed.

I have little excuse for extending my survey beyond the limits indicated by the term "knowledge". But I would not like to leave an impression that the description of the human spirit as "something which knows" can be accepted as the whole truth about its nature. It is not quite so narrow a description as "the observer"—the title bestowed by physical science. Consciousness has other functions besides those of a rather inefficient measuring machine; and knowledge may attain to other truths besides those which correlate sensory impressions. Yet, admitting the widest extension of the field of knowledge, its pursuit is only one of the activities proper to our self-fulfilment. The instinct to amass, perfect and glorify knowledge does not stand alone; it is akin to other instincts which claim the same acceptance, proceding alike from a mystic source welling up in our nature.

Even in science we realise that knowledge is not the only thing that counts. We allow ourselves to speak of the spirit of science. The rise of political systems hostile to science alarms us, not so much because of the check to the output of knowledge, but because of the suppression and perversion of the spirit of science. Deeper than any "form of thought" is a faith that creative activity signifies more than the thing it creates. In this faith, the crumbling of hard-won knowledge in the successive revolutions of science is not the continual tragedy that it seems.

In the age of reason, faith yet remains supreme; for reason is one of the articles of faith.

The problem of knowledge is an outer shell underneath which lies another philosophical problem—the problem of *values*. It cannot be pretended that the understanding and experience gained in the pursuit of scientific epistemology is of much avail here; but that is no reason for trying to persuade ourselves that the problem does not exist. A scientist should recognise in his philosophy—as he already recognises in his propaganda—that for the ultimate justification of his activity it is necessary to look, away from the knowledge itself, to a striving in man's nature, not to be justified of science or reason, for it is itself the justification of science, of reason, of art, of conduct. Of the relation of mysticism and science I have written elsewhere.

The danger of a broad view is that it is often a shallow view. We may claim for the epistemological outlook, limited though it may be, that it gives to the scientist a view broader than his traditional view without sacrificing depth. That it has been beneficial to the technical progress of physical science is undoubted. At the same time it gives a juster conception of the significance of physical knowledge in relation to philosophic thought—a perspective which neither exaggerates nor underrates the physical aspect of the world which forms a setting for the conscious experience of mankind. In particular, the realisation that physical knowledge is concerned only with structure points the way by which the conception of man as an element in a moral and spiritual order can be dovetailed into the conception of man as the plaything of the forces of the material world.

INDEX